"Commy"

THE MCFARLAND HISTORICAL BASEBALL LIBRARY

1. Cobb, Ty. *Busting 'Em and Other Big League Stories* (1914). 2003
2. Axelson, G.W. *"Commy": The Life Story of Charles A. Comiskey* (1919). 2003
3. Ellard, Harry. *Base Ball in Cincinnati: A History* (1907). 2004
4. Richter, Francis C. *Richter's History and Records of Base Ball, the American Nation's Chief Sport* (1914). 2005
5. Lanigan, Ernest J. *Baseball Cyclopedia* (1922). 2005
6. Evers, John J., and Hugh S. Fullerton. *Touching Second* (1910). 2005
7. Rice, Grantland. *Base-Ball Ballads* (1910). 2005
8. Claudy, C.H. *The Battle of Base-Ball* (1912). 2005
9. Kelly, Mike "King." *"Play Ball": Stories from the Diamond Field and Other Historical Writings about the 19th Century Hall of Famer* (1888). 2006.
10. Anonymous and Noah Brooks. *The Great Match* [1877] *and Our Base Ball Club* [1884]*: Two Novels from the Early Days of Base Ball,* volume editors Trey Strecker *and* Geri Strecker. 2010
11. Green, Guy W. *The Nebraska Indians* [1900] *and Fun and Frolic with an Indian Ball Team* [1907]*: Two Accounts of Baseball Barnstorming at the Turn of the Twentieth Century,* volume editor Jeffrey P. Beck. 2010
12. Salsinger, H.G. *Ty Cobb: Two Biographies—"Our Ty: Ty Cobb's Life Story" (1924) and "Which Was Greatest: Ty Cobb or Babe Ruth?" (1951),* volume editor William R. Cobb. 2012
13. Joss, Addie. *Addie Joss on Baseball: Collected Newspaper Columns and World Series Reports, 1907–1909,* compiled and annotated by Rich Blevins. 2012

"Commy"

The Life Story of Charles A. Comiskey

by G.W. Axelson

McFarland Historical Baseball Library, 2
Marty McGee *and* Gary Mitchem, *Editors*

McFarland & Company, Inc., Publishers
Jefferson, North Carolina, and London

Frontispiece: "The Old Roman."

Library of Congress Cataloguing-in-Publication Data

Axelson, G. W. (Gustaf W.)
"Commy" : the life story of Charles A. Comiskey / by G.W. Axelson.
[Marty McGee and Gary Mitchem, series editors]
p. cm. — (McFarland historical baseball library ; 2)
[Originally published: Chicago : Reilly & Lee, 1919]
Includes index.

ISBN 0-7864-1598-3 (softcover : 50# alkaline paper) ♾

1. Comiskey, Charles A. 2. Baseball team owners—United States—Biography. 3. Chicago White Sox (Baseball team) I. Title. II. Series.
GV865.C644A94 2003
796.357'092—dc21 2002155756

British Library cataloguing data are available

Cover image: Charles Comiskey

Manufactured in the United States of America

McFarland & Company, Inc., Publishers
Box 611, Jefferson, North Carolina 28640
www.mcfarlandpub.com

Table of Contents

Editors' Note

Charles Comiskey spent half a century in the big leagues as a successful player-manager and owner, his clubs winning nine pennants along the way. But a dark cloud perpetually hangs over those flags, blocking out the glory that would normally accompany such triumphs. That storm cloud is the 1919 Black Sox scandal, in which Comiskey is inextricably tangled, fair or not. It is true that he underpaid many of his players—in 1919 he paid Shoeless Joe Jackson $6,000 for his services, while Ty Cobb (the man who thought Jackson was the best player in baseball) was making $20,000 a year in Detroit—though some have pointed out that the White Sox payroll was not markedly lower than those of other clubs. Nevertheless, Comiskey's tight-fistedness is often cited as a principal cause of the 1919 World Series scandal. "Commy" suspected that the fix was on after the White Sox lost the first two games, and even implored his old (but soon to be ex-) friend, American League president Ban Johnson, to suspend the Series, but the tide of history could not be dammed. The scandal affected him deeply and bitterly, and he never really could escape its shadow until his death in 1931. Eight years later Charles Comiskey was posthumously honored with a spot in the executives' wing of the National Baseball Hall of Fame.

Editors' Note

Commy told his life story to Chicago sportswriter Gustav W. Axelson in 1918, and the Reilly & Lee Co. published the biography the next year, only months before the infamous World Series that would permanently change the way readers approached the book. After news of the fix broke in 1920, "*Commy*" became a text that might be scoured for some hint of what was imminent. But there is little in the book that foreshadows the events of 1919—in Chapter 1 Axelson says that Comiskey "confesses to only one gamble—the invasion of Chicago with his White Sox"—but historians of the game will find much valuable insight here on the rise of baseball in the Windy City, Comiskey's playing career (as an innovative first baseman), his long stint as St. Louis Browns player-manager (which included four straight pennants from 1885 to 1888), his helping Johnson form the American League, and his keeping the White Sox a family-owned franchise for nearly 60 years.

Surprisingly, this is the only biography of Comiskey ever published. As Axelson notes at the conclusion of Chapter VI, "Comiskey has refrained in the past from writing a line of autobiography, and it is only by piecing together scraps of information from different sources that his real worth as a player and leader may be arrived at." But, Axelson does allow "The Old Roman" to speak for himself briefly in the last seven pages of the book. Here Comiskey comes across as humble and earnest, concluding his message with, "What I have tried to do [in baseball] has been my level best."

McFarland is pleased to bring the reader this reprint edition of one of the earliest and most important baseball biographies. Copies of the original hardcover edition are exceedingly rare, thus the need to make Comiskey's pre–Black Sox story more accessible to baseball researchers.

Marty McGee
Gary Mitchem

♦ CHAPTER I ♦

Baseball or Bricks

High lights in Comiskey's career—Libertys claim him first—World loses indifferent teamster but gains a great ball player—Born in the greatest baseball city—The original White Stockings of 1870—Two jolts for Cincinnati Red Stockings.

In the Centennial year of 1876 there appeared on Chicago's diamonds a tall and lanky youth known to local fame as a pitcher. He brought into the game a sinewy right arm, a pair of speedy legs and a strong individuality. An eventful career of forty-three years has well-nigh robbed him of all but the last. But this individuality sets him apart from others now as it did in '76. Were it otherwise there would be no occasion to enter upon the life story of Charles Albert Comiskey, known to millions as a player, manager, club-owner and man.

Cast in a daring mold he scorned precedent and cut loose from tradition to the advantage of the sport which he has helped to make America's own. As a player and manager he blazed the way for a new game on the ball field. He pried the first baseman loose from the bag to which he had been anchored since baseball was young and he himself set a pace in the position that has not been surpassed.

Comiskey made a mobile force of the infield and his aggressiveness compelled the overhauling of the playing rules. He turned baseball from the channels of evolution into those of revolution and while still in the flush of youth became its greatest exponent. He brought four successive pennants to St. Louis. He has given to Chicago as many. He topped the eight with three world's titles: eleven in all—a record without a parallel in the sport.

Becoming master of his own fortunes he sought out new worlds to conquer. His energy, daring and judgment became proverbial. "Comiskey tours" came to have a new meaning in the peregrinations of ball teams. De Luxe specials supplanted the day coach. He was the first to pitch his training camp in foreign lands. His autumnal jaunts into the wilds of the northern woods at the head of the faithful, marked the peak in hospitality.

Having explored every nook and corner of his native land he looked beyond the seas, circled the globe, and the opportunity was afforded the elect of the earth to see the White Sox and Giants in action.

Being the champion hard loser of the universe he took chances that others dodged. His optimism, the heritage of his race, saw him through. New ventures became commonplace. Paying $50,000 for a ball player was a mere formality. The building of a half-a-million-dollar baseball plant was a matter of bookkeeping—dependent on the balance in the bank.

As for his principal hazards, Comiskey himself confesses to only one gamble—the invasion of Chicago with his White Sox. On this he staked everything he possessed and in addition gave a mortgage on the future. Within a few years he was in sole possession of a major league ball club—the only player who had ever risen from the ranks to that distinction. He is the only American or National league owner without a partner in a business where turnstiles alone dictate the size of the bank account.

I. Baseball or Bricks

Around the council table his fellow owners respected his judgment from the beginning. Rival magnates insisted that he was the brains of the American League, but regardless of opinions all came to love him for what he was—a man. His physical makeup and personal traits made him the "Old Roman" to the millions who watched him as leader of the St. Louis Browns. To his pals, who are legion, he was, and is, simply "Commy," and by that appellation he will be best known to posterity.

Comiskey's entrance into baseball did not differ greatly from that of other boys of his age. He learned the game on the prairies as did the rest but unlike others he chose it as a calling while to the majority of his team-mates it never was anything but a pastime. A load of brick proved the turning point. An irate father unwittingly aided him in making his decision.

It was on a summer's day in 1876 that the future owner of world's champions encountered his destiny at the corner of Jackson and Laflin streets in Chicago. From the driver's seat of a brick wagon he noticed that the Libertys' pitcher, trying out for an important contest with the Franklins, was having the life hammered out of him, on a nearby diamond. Dropping the reins, as he hopped down from his perch, the batters soon were swinging at different curves.

Two miles to the northeast there were loud calls for bricks. Chicago's City Hall could not rise from the ashes of '71 without them. Telephones not being available in those days it was not until the shank-end of the try-out that the mystery was solved. It was about that period in our national sport that "Honest John" Comiskey, alderman from the Seventh Ward and Democratic leader, found the charioteer of the load of brick on the point of striking out the side.

The discovery and surprise were mutual but each kept his own counsel. The father swung himself up behind the bays and departed. The son finished the game and went home, but with some trepidation.

He surmised that he had come to the parting of the ways. It would have to be baseball or bricks. At the family council that night the world lost an indifferent teamster but gained a great ball player.

Forty-one years later the Chicago City Council, in a meeting assembled, on the very spot towards which that load of bricks had been headed, passed the following resolution:

> Whereas, Our favorites, the White Sox, have won the pennant in the American League and with it the right to compete in a series with the New York Giants for the World's Baseball Championship, therefore be it
>
> Resolved, that the City Council of the City of Chicago hereby extends its congratulations to Charles A. Comiskey and to the members of his baseball team for their splendid victory, and its best wishes that the White Sox may win further honors for themselves, their owner, and Chicago, by showing New York's team that the "I Will" spirit is not to be denied.

The span measures the time between the unfinished journey from the brick-yard at Twenty-second and Laflin streets to the corner of LaSalle and Washington, and the completed pennant race in 1917. Comiskey was the headliner in both incidents. Tack on seventeen years and you have his age at that time, counting from August 15, 1859.

Important changes have marked that period of three score years. Baseball has had its share. At Comiskey's birth the game was just discarding its swaddling clothes. As he grew to manhood it could still be considered a novelty. Critics might disagree as to the newness of the pastime, accepting the verdict of history that it had been played as early as 1839, or even before that year, yet it was not until the early Seventies that it was generally recognized as America's "national" sport.

I. Baseball or Bricks

Prior to the Civil War days there were sporadic attempts to organize teams but it was not until the late Sixties that the sport assumed a sectional character. What contests there had been were purely of local interest. The Knickerbocker Club of New York was organized in 1845 and the first match game on record was played a year later at Hoboken, New Jersey. It may be noticed that through the "ace" scoring which prevailed in those days, only four innings were required by the "New York Club," a pick-up nine, to get the first decision.

As early as 1866 the sporting authorities of that period considered baseball of national importance, even though no intersectional leagues had been organized and no schedules drawn up. The following is taken from Charles A. Peverelly's "Book of American Pastimes," published at New York, 1866:

> The game of baseball has now become, beyond question, the leading feature of the outdoor sports of the United States, and to account for its truly proud position, there are many and sufficient reasons. It is a game which is peculiarly suited to the American temperament and disposition; the nine innings are played in the brief space of two and a half hours or less. From the moment the first striker takes his position and poses his bat it has excitement and vim about it until the last hand is put out in the ninth inning. There is no delay or suspense about it from the beginning to end; and, even if one feels disposed to leave the ground, temporarily, he will generally waive this desire, especially if it is a close contest, from fear of missing some good point or clever effort of the trial.
>
> An American assemblage cannot be kept in one locality for the period of two or three hours, without being offered something above the ordinary run of excitement and attraction....
>
> Wherever established it (the game) has quickly had the sentiment and good feeling of the community with it, and with

> scarcely an effort, achieved solid popularity. Having no debasing attributes and being worthy of the presence of the good and refined, it has everywhere been countenanced and encouraged by our best citizens: and, of the thousands who gather at important matches, we have always noted with sincere gratification that the ladies constituted an honored proportion.

It is to be regretted that Alderman Comiskey had not perused Peverelly's book at the time of the halted brick wagon. Had it formed part of his library he possibly would have developed a more lenient attitude towards the pastime and kept his son at home. In that case Milwaukee, Elgin, Dubuque, St. Louis, Cincinnati and St. Paul, would not have had the opportunity to boast of the prowess of the lean twirler and first baseman.

Although the historical side of the sport will only be lightly touched upon in these pages the genesis of the game in Chicago will be discussed at some length as it has a direct bearing on the later activities of the man who grew up with the modern game and who probably has done more than any other to put it on a firm footing. Fate decreed that Comiskey should first see light at Union and Maxwell streets, in the greatest baseball city on earth. He had the advantage of growing up in a section of the country that afforded its "future greats" plenty of elbow room, eventually enough for nearly 1,000 teams, amateur, semipro and full blown professional.

Alfred H. Spink, author of "The National Game," a valuable treatise on the sport, contends that "next to New York, Chicago is the greatest baseball city in America." Mr. Spink, who was born in Chicago and who became a citizen of St. Louis by adoption, may be pardoned for his impartial but debatable assertion, as Gotham seems to have had the edge on the city by the Lake in the length of its baseball history.

Charles A. Comiskey, however, is also a Chicagoan by birth.

He has been a temporary sojourner in the Mound City, in New York, and in fact, in most every other city and hamlet, in and out of the country, where baseball has been played. The "Old Roman" is not given to extravagant speech and his opinion should have some weight. He says:

> Chicago is the greatest of all baseball cities. I make no exception although I have been treated well wherever I have been. It is the greatest city because the fans will stick to a loser season after season. I have had my share of defeats so I should know. Boston and St. Louis come next; in fact I believe I would give the palm to the latter, as the fans in Boston have shown themselves slightly mercurial.
>
> A winner in New York is apt to wear out the turnstiles but the "average" crowd is not up to the standard with a loser. At home here my team has played to 12,000 and 15,000 on a week-day with the club in the second division. That is the test of loyalty.

It may be surmised that Chicago was loyal from the start but historians are a little hazy as to what actually happened in the early days. A team called the "Unions" played town ball somewhere on the prairies as far back as 1856. In 1859 the Excelsiors break into print in "The Spirit of the Times," published in New York. A communication from Chicago, dated May 1, states:

> The baseball clubs of this city are in active preparation for their season, which promises to be a lively one. There are three or four clubs here. The Excelsiors is the most prominent one, and is one of the pioneer clubs, having been in existence for a year or more. It was the first club to adopt the new style game played under the rules and regulations of the National Association (organized in New York, 1857) known as the New York

> game. The Excelsiors make a nice appearance on the ball field in their new uniforms, which consist of long white pants and white shirts made of English flannel. Their practice days are Tuesday and Friday.

This was the modest beginning of baseball journalism as practiced three months before "Commy" first saw light. Fifty-eight years later the wires from New York carried into a single Chicago newspaper office on a single night 20,000 words on how the Chicago White Sox defeated the Giants for the World's Baseball Championship.

The Civil War put a quietus to baseball in Chicago as it did the country over, and it was not until 1865 that the game again began to show signs of life. Then a new Excelsior team was put in the field with the Atlantics as their strongest rivals. After trimming each other and mowing down less pretentious opponents three years were spent in strengthening these teams, unconscious of the need Chicago would have of them in repelling a coming invasion by the Cincinnati Red Stockings.

The Red Stockings were out-and-out professionals. The Excelsiors and Atlantics were amateurs. Taking on the Excelsiors first, June 21, 1868, the Reds tumbled the Chicagoans 43 to 22 and on the following day the Atlantics fell 28 to 9.

The defeats were most important to baseball in Chicago as they served to bring to the front the original White Stockings, predecessors of the White Sox today, in name at least. The team was organized in the fall of 1869 for the purpose of putting the city on the baseball map. In reality it was built to take the measure of the Red Stockings, who had just finished the season without losing a game, a record which never has been equaled.

Opposite: **Comiskey at the opening of his $1,000,000 baseball park in 1910.**

PHOTO BY
BURKE & ATWELL
CHICAGO

"Commy"

After the Reds' visit in 1868 baseball in Chicago boomed as never before and teams sprang up like mushrooms. Diamonds girdled the city, the limits of which were not as far-flung in those days as at present, being marked on the north by Division street, on the south by Twelfth, with the "farthest West" at the intersection of Ogden avenue and Madison street. The city boasted of only one enclosed field but these were the days of real sport and "future greats" were far more contented among the tin cans around Bull's Head Tavern than are the "fifteen thousand dollar beauties" arrayed in championship raiment.

Among the teams which battled on the West Side prairies at the time the curtain was rising on the pastime were the Libertys, Actives, Mutuals and Neversweats. The principal team on the North Side was the Atlantics which later became known as the Aetnas and which wound up as the Franklins. The Pastimes were considered the class of the South Side while the future loop district sheltered the Excelsiors.

The survival of the fittest being the law of the prairies, certain teams with the best backing in bone and muscle finally gravitated towards fixed spots and thus we find in the late Sixties the Actives established at Lake and Ada streets, the Libertys at Madison and Western, the Mutuals at Van Buren and Leavitt streets and the Pastimes at South Chicago.

At this period there also appeared upon the scene the Dreadnaughts, who did not belie their name as they nearly made a clean sweep of opposing teams. The pitching prowess of "Cherokee" Fisher, an importation from the East, and the skill of Ole Olson at first base were mainly responsible for a long list of Dreadnaught victories.

Great players graduated from these rough diamonds and not a few attained national fame. From the Aetnas came such stars as Jack

Carbine, first baseman of the Louisville National League team; Jimmy Hallinan, short stop of the original White Stockings; Paddy Quinn, one of the first receivers to catch close up to the batter without mask or gloves; Hughey Reid, a noted Chicago pitcher; Paddy Lynch, great first baseman, and Graves, a star fielder.

The Foley Brothers, Tom, John, Charles and William, with the Actives, were all sterling players; Mike Brennock, W. B. Lapham and McClelland, were others. Em Gross, who later became the catcher on the champion Providence team, was with the Pastimes as was Bill Phillips, later star first sacker on Cleveland's crack team.

The Libertys turned out such players as Ike Fleming, a corking catcher in his days and, incidentally Comiskey's first manager; Mike Hayes, noted pitcher; the O'Day Brothers, Dan, James and Henry, the latter "Hank" of the National League umpire staff, the dean of his profession. The name "O'Day," however, is not to be found in the early lineups. It was plain "Day," the excision of the "O" being due to the elder O'Day's opinion of the game, which coincided with that entertained by Alderman Comiskey.

Individual objections to the "frivolous pastime" did not, however, prevent the organization of the White Stockings, who were backed by business men prominent in the city's affairs. Native talent had predominated in the lineups of the Excelsiors and the Atlantics and their defeats by the Reds had been a distinct blow to local pride. After the Red Stockings of 1869 had swept the country from Frisco to New York, the exigencies of the occasion demanded heroic measures and sentimental considerations were thrown into the discard. The country was combed for players and this team resulted:

William H. Craver, catcher; Levi Meyerle, Edward Pinkham and Tom Burns, pitchers; James McAtee, first base; Jimmy Wood, second base; Meyerle, third base; Charley Hodes, short stop; Edgar Cuthbert, left field; Fred Treacy, center; and Clipper Flynn, right field.

After much strategy on both sides the two teams were matched and clashed at Dexter Park, September 7, 1870, a memorable occasion in the baseball annals of Chicago. Opposed to the White Stockings were this galaxy of Red Stocking stars, perhaps the greatest collection of players which the country had seen up to that time:

Asa Brainard, pitcher; Douglas Allison, catcher; Charles Gould, first base; Charles Sweasy, second base; George Wright, short stop; Fred Waterman, third base; Andrew Leonard, left; Harry Wright, captain and center, and Calvan McVey, right field. Richard Hurley was the substitute.

As of historical interest it might be pointed out that the salaries ranged from $1,400 to $800. George Wright received the former figure. His brother Harry was in receipt of $200 less.

The chronicler of the day indulged in gladiatorial similes, and judging from all accounts, everybody got his money's worth. The score, 10 to 6 in favor of the White Stockings, was considered close enough to call for another game and the Reds returned on October 13 for one more drubbing, this time 16 to 13. The historian had this to say about the teams:

> No finer looking teams have ever taken the field than were these two. Every player of each team was in perfect condition. Discipline and good order were in evidence, too, the men appearing in clean and showy uniforms.
>
> The Chicagos wore white flannel caps, shirts and stockings and blue trousers while the Cincinnati boys were dressed in white shirts and trousers with red caps and stockings. Each and every player seemed to be in the very pink of condition and each of the two games was magnificently played and contested.

The fact that ropes had to be stretched around the field was ample proof that Chicago was taking to the game. The civic spirit manifested in the backing of the victors left no doubt in the minds of the critics that the White Stockings had located in the right town. Taking into consideration the handicaps under which the "avengers" labored they made a good start towards advertising the future motto of Chicago. They had no grounds to practice on in the spring of 1870 and it was not until 1871 that they found a home, Chicago's first league grounds being located at the foot of Lake street, east of Michigan avenue.

In the meantime the White Stockings had joined the National Association of Professional Baseball Players, finishing third among the clubs left at the end of the season of 1871. In the fall of that year came the great fire and it was curtains for the game until 1874 when the league was again honored by a White Stocking team with a fifth place berth at the close. In 1875, the last year of the association, they were sixth. Promotion was rapid after that, as in the following year the National League was organized and Chicago took its rightful place among the great in the baseball world.

♦ CHAPTER II ♦

The Game Becomes a Business

The spirit of the West—"Revolving" becomes popular—"Honest John" Comiskey—Cobwebs on plumber's tools—Story of 10 percent and a $15,000 gate—Comiskey becomes a "regular"—Baseball and books—Ted Sullivan makes a discovery.

Up to 1871 Chicago had conducted a defensive campaign in baseball. Few teams went outside the city limits, although, then as now, they were ready to meet all comers. Local pride dictated the strength of the teams and it is not on record that a single combination was organized for show. There was no such silk-stockinged aggregation as the Knickerbockers of New York, whose prominence was accentuated more by gastronomic performances than by feats on the ball field.

There is no intention to cast a slur on the old "Knicks" as they did their part in laying the foundation for our national sport, yet, there was a vast difference, in the early days, between baseball in New York and Chicago. The social side had equal or greater weight than the playing end in the East while in the West it was all "the game."

On Chicago's fields, from the waving prairies on the west to the lake, from the morasses on the south to the wild-woods on the north, all were equal, once in baseball uniform. There was no distinction on account of birth and breeding, and that spirit prevailed, to a large extent, in the entire territory west of the Alleghanies. Batting and fielding averages alone decided the fitness of the plumber and the dandy. This made the transition from amateurism to professionalism open and above board as against the complaisant attitude of the East where semi-professionals and out and out "pros" masqueraded as amateurs, to the detriment of the game.

The Cincinnati Red Stockings made the effete East blush when their pay checks were made public property. So ingrained was the amateur idea, even up to the late Sixties, that the Nationals of Washington insisted on waving aside all gate receipts during their memorable trip in 1867. Still, promising players were offered lucrative positions, both privately and with the government, could they but see their way clear to join the invincible team of the nation's capital.

In Chicago, however, the question of amateurs and professionals was never raised. For several years there was no chance to be anything else than the former as the receipts collected on unenclosed fields were not enough to defray the expenses to and from the games. When necessity arose the city went out and bought a winner openly, instead of surreptitiously, as was the fashion elsewhere and, with the organization of the White Stockings, baseball in Chicago flourished as a "business," a calling as honorable as any of the other professions.

Certain purists might regret that, as a national sport, it did not follow the lines of cricket in England, where professionalism was and is subordinated to amateurism, in theory if not actually. Early promoters of the game held that it always would retain its amateur status but they failed to take into account the human equation, the spirit of rivalry which it engendered and the will to excel. Had it remained only a healthgiving pastime and had it never functioned as an amusement these hopes might have been realized.

Thriving on competition, the sport drew to itself the red-blooded youth of the land, because it not only served as an outlet to physical exuberance but it was the nearest approach to "peacetime war" which, in turn, was translated into victories and defeats. As the average American is a hard loser, rivalry increased wherever a ball was put into play. The basic principle of the game being centered in decisions it was but natural that both sides should strain every nerve to win. The defeated team would naturally scour its own neighborhood, after a losing battle, for talent to strengthen its attack. The victors of to-day would, in turn, become the losers of to-morrow and the recruiting would continue until the time when one or the other had combed the vicinity clean or, by a succession of victories, would have arrogated to itself undisputed mastery on the village diamond.

As the circle increased in size, and the exigencies of the occasion demanded, offers to exchange allegiance became more tempting. A bag of marbles, a share in the "swag," or any other bait may have marked the crossing of the line but whatever the lure, the player had become a professional, in theory at least. It was then up to the ethically inclined to draw the distinction between the boy whose remuneration had been extracted from the community treasure house and the man who succumbed to a $5,000 contract.

The "revolving" of players, as it was called in the early days of the game, was perfectly natural and, without it, the game probably never would have become national. It was necessary to its development but it was death to amateurism. There may be some consolation in the fact that from the ashes of the latter rose the only simon-pure national professional game—a pastime which has stood the test of time and which is to-day the squarest sport on earth.

The great majority of teams in the west were, of course, amateur both from choice and necessity—from choice because possibly they could afford it; from necessity because of the lack of a "gate." Professionalism carried with it no disgrace as it did in most of the eastern centers, and the west, as soon as the game had become solidly organized, made baseball a real profession, with no stigma attached to its practice.

As late as 1871 and, after the Cincinnati Red Stockings had popularized the professional end of the sport, Harry Wright, the former leader of this peerless aggregation, went to Boston to organize a regular league team. Such was the prejudice against "pros" that Wright did not dare to openly announce his intentions of having none but paid members on the roster. Instead, the subterfuge of the counting room, the railroad office and the political berth was resorted to. The fallacy and hypocrisy of this procedure was pointed out to the progressive manager and he abandoned the experiment and, with some misgivings, boldly announced the signing of a team to play ball. The Hub fans took kindly to the innovation and in time the rest of the seaboard fell in line.

In Chicago substantial business men tagged the professional game with respectability by the universal backing of the White Stockings. The city dug into its jeans for the money necessary to build a team that could take the measure of the Red Stockings and it has adhered to this effective method ever since. Win or lose, any combination with a Chicago emblem has been supported as in no other city in the country. This spirit naturally had its influence on the youth and contributed not a little to the reputation which the sport has enjoyed since the first ball bounded over the virgin soil.

It was into such an atmosphere that the willowy youth, hailing from the neighborhood of Union and Maxwell streets, was ushered in the early Seventies. In the same wholesome surroundings he is rounding out his wonderful career. To the average business man, engrossed with the affairs of his particular calling, the gradual steps from batboy to president and owner of the world's champions may not in themselves seem unusual in this age of super-achievements but to the millions of fans who have followed the fortunes of Charles A. Comiskey they have a world of meaning. Within the period of "Commy's" manhood is embraced the complete development of the marvelous game in which he is one of the most commanding figures and the services rendered to the sport by him have been equaled by few and surpassed by no one.

Comiskey's influence on the game surpassed his actual accomplishments, important as these were, especially from the time he took charge of the old St. Louis Browns to the present, a period of 35 years. From the bat-toting days of '69 down to the swivel chair stage of 1919 his life has been an open book to the millions who have perused the pages of the daily press. During all that time the finger of suspicion never has been pointed in his direction.

What is even more remarkable, considering the fact that "Commy" has figured in public print for well over a third of a century, he has yet to make a request for a "retraction." To anyone versed in the intricacies of newspaper reporting and the numberless controversies which our national sport develops this record of the player-magnate is unique. Add to this the fact that the esteem of his fellow players, managers and owners is as great as that entertained by the army of fans, and the distinction is complete.

The superlatives which might be applicable to his later years have, so far as is known, no place in the description of "Commy's" boyhood days.

Young Comiskey was just like any other youngster who had to be useful around the house. However, he developed strategy early, an attribute called into requisition in order that he might satisfy his craving for outdoor sports. His father, John Comiskey, was of that type of man who abhorred idleness and frowned on play. He insisted that work and education were the prime requisites to success and he decided that his children—there were seven boys and one girl—should have both.

The elder Comiskey came from a sturdy stock. In rectitude and sternness he might have felt at home among the Puritans of New England had his forebears been from any other spot than County Cavan, Ireland. The following is a pen picture of him furnished by Henry F. Donovan, editor and publisher of Chicago, who knew him well:

> John Comiskey, the father of the popular baseball king, Charles A. Comiskey, was for many years one of Chicago's leading citizens, and one of the men who helped to make Chicago great. John Comiskey was the first president of the city council of

Comiskey as manager and first-baseman of the St. Louis Browns.

> Chicago under the old city charter which provided for that office. For eleven years he was an alderman and a useful and honored one. He was first elected in 1859 from the old Tenth ward, still representing it when its number was changed to the Seventh and still its representative when it became the Eighth. This ward was one of the most respectable in the city and was peopled by the flower of the Irish race in America. Mr. Comiskey was a great representative for it and was honored by all classes. He was courtly in manner, eloquent in speech, honest and aggressive in all things, and always a gentleman.
>
> John Comiskey was born in Crosserlough, County Cavan, Ireland, and came to America in 1848, settling in New Haven, Connecticut, where he went into the lumber business. Not pleased with the East and its opportunities, he came to Chicago in 1852 and for a time had charge of the incoming freight on the Chicago, Rock Island and Pacific Railroad. He afterwards became superintendent of shipments at the Pittsburgh, Fort Wayne and Chicago cattle yards in Chicago—the Union Stock Yards not then being in existence.
>
> He was deputy United States internal revenue collector under President Andrew Johnson and was clerk of the Cook County Board for several years.

Although living in the "easy" age of politics when brown stone fronts usually followed a few years in office, he died in 1900, the year that his son put an American League team into Chicago, in the same modest dwelling in which he had spent his life.

Unlike his son the father considered the West Side as the center of Chicago and there he married Miss Annie Kearns of Albany, New York, in 1852. Of the family of eight Charles was the third, a favorite of the mother whom he remembers as ever ready to take his part when chided by the father for his unseemly attachment to the "frivolous" game the boys were playing on the lots.

Although the elder Comiskey was willing and anxious to give his children an education he was also insistent on a trade. He argued that the former might become a liability but there could be no question of a handicraft being an asset. Thus the future owner of champions was first set to massage lead pipes under the eye of one Hogan, who rejoiced in the title of "master plumber."

This arrangement worked well enough in the winter when the snow was on the ground but with the first sign of spring the cobwebs settled on the plumber's tools. As these accumulated Comiskey senior decided to give his offspring a front seat on the brickwagon where we have already discovered him, as he deserted it for the diamond. His trait of making up his mind on the instant cropped out then as it did years later.

In the spring of 1917 Comiskey sat at the dinner table in the Rice Hotel at Houston, Texas. It was shortly before the United States declared war on Germany but at a time when the country expected the momentous decision to be taken. I laid a telegram from the editor of the Chicago newspaper, with which I was connected, before him. It read:

"Please ask Mr. Comiskey if he will donate 10 percent of his gate receipts to the American Red Cross."

The "Old Roman" fumbled for his glasses a moment, couldn't find them, and said: "What is it all about?"

He was told and after a pause of, perhaps, fifteen seconds, replied: "Tell the editor that it will be a pleasure to give the money. But is 10 percent enough? I don't think it is. I owe my country everything I have and it can call on me for every cent I possess. To offer all is the least we can do, we who are too old to go to the front, should that become necessary."

After the answer had been formulated he tapped his fingers on the table for an instant and a shade of disappointment came over his face as he remarked: "I should have thought about that myself."

A similar incident occurred during the playing season in 1918. The Chicago women in charge of entertainment of soldiers and sailors needed a hostess' house in Grant Park. They went to B. B. Johnson, president of the American League, who put the matter in my hands. Knowing that Mr. Comiskey was being "touched" for every kind of charity I hesitated when the suggestion was made that I "see what Mr. Comiskey could do." However, I went and he was asked to donate a percentage of the gate receipts of a Chicago-Cleveland game.

As at Houston, the canvasser was floored when, as soon as the owner of the Sox had found out what it was for, he said:

"A percentage is not enough. You must have my entire share of the gate receipts and I will try to make it a big day."

With the co-operation of James C. Dunn, owner of the Cleveland team, and a sportsman of the Comiskey type, $15,000 was realized.

On that summer evening in 1876 it was more of a momentous decision that "Commy" made than parting with the gate receipts two score years later. A career was at stake. Perhaps he did not appreciate that it was for life, but it would have made no difference. After he had made up his mind, it was settled, and, as he fondly hoped, his good right arm would see him through. He did not figure on that kink in his throwing "wing" which developed in a couple of years.

He was seventeen years of age at the time and, except at brief intervals, the cottage on Union and Maxwell streets saw him no more. He cut home ties for good in 1877 even though he was hazy in his mind as to the next move, but having specialized in the national game, to baseball he turned.

He had achieved the distinction of being change pitcher for the Libertys, a team which was cutting wide swaths on the prairie diamonds. Perhaps, like other boys of his age, he conjured up his triumphal return to the old homestead and the deference to be paid him by the "cop" on the beat, who had chased him off proscribed lots after an unlucky foul through a neighbor's window had terminated the game. Possibly, he even cogitated on the chance of converting the "old man" to the sport, but he must have had his doubts about this as the incident connected with his try-out was still fresh in his mind.

"Commy's" debut as a "regular" followed shortly after he had clamped on the brakes on the wagon in Jackson street. After several overtures he had been given a trial on the Libertys, whose manager, Ike Fleming, had decided that he would do as a pitcher. The Libertys had arranged to meet the Franklin team, another strong amateur combination. It was with many misgivings that Comiskey went into the box, but the score of 2 to 1 in favor of the Libertys confirmed him in his belief that, perhaps, he could make a living at something else besides swinging the curry comb.

This game, Comiskey's first regular contest, was played in Lincoln Park. On the team which backed up the youthful pitcher were William Healy, catcher and later alderman; Ike Fleming, manager and first base and still in the newspaper business as he was then; William McGrady, second base, for many years connected with the Cook County treasurer's office; Johnny Fitzgibbons, third base; George Eddy, of Eddy's Foundry Company, short stop; Dan O'Day, Charles McGrady and Mike Hayes, outfielders.

Professionalism had thrived for several years in Chicago, but young Comiskey did not dare to aspire to a place on the crack teams, which now included the first Chicago National League team, an aggregation which was to win the initial championship of the parent organization, and one from which he was later to wrest the world's title. Through a knot hole in the fence he watched such artists as Spalding, Anson, White, McVey, Hines, Barnes and others and decided that he didn't "belong," but would seek an opening with less pretentious company.

From the time he was in short trousers at St. Ignatius College "Commy" had combined the art of pitching with the more abstruse problems in mathematics and kindred studies so, when he was promoted to St. Mary's College in Kansas, he had arrived at that stage where the college director considered him good enough to lead the freshman team as captain. His older brother Jim was catcher on another nine at school while he himself frequently took his turn behind the batter.

One Ted Sullivan seems to have cut the biggest swath on the St. Mary's grounds, the Ted who later in life became the greatest organizer of baseball clubs and leagues in the history of the game. Ted was shortstop and occasionally took a fling at pitching. When Ted was pitching he wanted Charles as battery mate.

"I picked out Comiskey," related Ted, "because I considered him the smartest kid on the teams. One incident will show how quickly, even in those days, he grasped an opportunity. I noticed that a runner on third was taking a rather big lead. Comiskey signalled for a certain ball. I shook my head. He signalled for another and I repeated. Finally I left the box, all the time upbraiding him because of his bonehead strategy. He never said a word but met me half way, and still bawling him out I slipped him the ball while I returned to the mound.

"All set behind the bat and Comiskey whipped the ball to third nailing the runner by ten feet. I did not tell him what to do. I simply wanted to find out if he could think for himself. From that time on I began to have respect for Charles, and he was only a kid at that."

The admiration seems to have been mutual and the acquaintance formed had important consequences for baseball.

II. The Game Becomes a Business

In due time Comiskey was transferred to the Christian Brothers College at Prairie du Chien, where, in the opinion of Comiskey senior, the opportunity for studying baseball was on a less extensive scale.

♦ CHAPTER III ♦

That Hole in the Fence

What became of Sir Thomas Shaughnessy's $50—Comiskey enters on a career of speed—The "cop" and the pass—New wrinkles in slides—He shows the world how to play first base—Helps to win a pennant—Appears at Sportsman's Park—"He will do" is verdict.

After the Comiskey family council Charles remembered Ted and turned to him for advice. Sullivan at this time was the manager of the Alerts in Milwaukee, his native city. Ted needed a pitcher and Comiskey was engaged. The man who furnished the money for the uniforms and equipment was Thomas G. Shaughnessy, now Sir Thomas, former president of the Canadian Pacific Railroad and during the war, purchasing agent for the British government.

There was a wooden fence around the Alerts' grounds but a hole on one side made a free gate to anyone who cared to enter. Sullivan's pleadings moved the backer of the team to contribute $50 for lumber. Some time later, the hole being still there, Shaughnessy accosted the manager.

"Why, the $50 you gave me," said the urbane Ted, "I handed to that lanky pitcher over there. He needed the money as much as I needed his services and, besides, Charles Comiskey is a friend of mine."

Shaughnessey watched the curves which the young man handed up and allowed that the manager had been wise in his choice. He jotted down $50 for "general expenses"—the Alerts being an amateur team, salary couldn't figure in the amount.

"That $50 for a month's work was really the first money I ever earned as a ball player," said Comiskey, in relating the incident. As he was talking he thumbed a check book on his desk, the stub from one showing that he had paid a certain player now on the White Sox team at the rate of $83 a day or $33 more than the "Old Roman" received for a month's work.

With the advent of winter Comiskey buckled down to a useful trade but on the coming of spring he said good-bye, to return as the undisputed head of his own house. He moved to Elgin to become the pitcher on the watch factory team. At Milwaukee his success had been only mediocre as Sullivan was unable to find a catcher who could hold him. To guard against this contingency he took his own battery mate, Rudolph Kemmler, to Elgin with him, and such was the pitching of Comiskey and the backing he received that the watch factory team did not lose a single game, a record which, in a small way, matched that of the Red Stockings eight years before.

Although Comiskey, during many a season, failed to get the requisite speed out of his ball club, he himself started at a pace which few were able to follow. He doted on speed. To his way of thinking, no pitcher could show enough of it, while his catchers insisted that he had entirely too much. It was the same on the bases. With his team behind, the runners all looked like ice wagons to the peppery youth from Chicago. If in the lead he expected everybody to practice sprinting for the next game. He was a glutton for totals. Never was the score big enough. He could always show after the game that they should have had another tally or two and, to his way of thinking, players were on the field to run up the score.

That Comiskey never let up in his pace either on or off the ball field, can be corroborated by a crossing policeman on Michigan avenue, at Thirty-fifth street in Chicago. Here is where "Commy" usually turns to go to his ball park.

The boss of the White Sox had known the "cop" for years and annually presented him with a season pass to the games. The fact that "Commy's" chauffeur was in the habit of taking the corner on two wheels had nothing to do with it, but at length Casey began to have his doubts. Flagging the hurrying magnate one day the policeman apologetically approached the auto and delivered this ultimatum:

"Mr. Comiskey, if you don't slow up on my beat I will have to give you back my pass."

Being unable to take a trimming with equanimity, "Commy" early acquired the reputation of being the hardest loser wherever he appeared. He fought fairly, but he never could get it out of his head that Fate had picked out the other side for the doormat. Providence, he figured, was always on his own side, but he also made it a rule to be helpful in presenting the strongest lineup and, if this was not feasible, to take advantage of every weakness of the opposition.

As a kid pitcher Comiskey depended on speed. Later he added an effective out-curve, a ball hard to hit, according to his contemporaries. Using an underhand delivery his height did not give him that assistance which it does to the overthrow, but there was no question about his effectiveness. He had the batter under his thumb most of the time and no slugger faced him the second time but he knew what to feed him.

There has been a difference of opinion whether "Commy" classed among the really great pitchers. He himself says that his arm gave out before he had a chance to find out. Those who played with him claim that the fact that he seldom could get a backstop to hold him influenced him to quit the box before his time. One thing is certain. Regardless of the condition of his salary wing his head would have made it a fifty-fifty proposition for the batter for some years.

Being a pitcher he could not be expected to lead the batting order, but at that he was usually placed pretty close to the top. He was no Tip O'Neill in slugging, but no pitcher took liberties with him the second time. He seldom put the ball over the fence, but instead devoted his energies to getting the twirler in a hole. Pinch hitting was his long suit.

Not having time to develop on the pitcher's mound, it was his work on the bases and in fielding which became distinctive. He was fast on his feet but he could hardly be regarded as a "ten second man." Yet there were few who had the art of base-stealing down to a finer science. Getting on, he was a runner not to be trifled with. If the chances were even he was certain to advance a base or two. If they were less he was smart enough to wait for the inevitable break.

It was risky to slide in the early days of the game on any except the best kept diamonds. Feet first and it might mean a broken leg or a twisted ankle. Head first and it was "raw meat" from the shoulders to the hips. With Comiskey it was the latter and many give him the credit of originating the trick. Bill Gleason—the "Bill" of the Browns—writes that he had never seen anyone go head first before Comiskey came along and taught this particular "hook" to the boys.

"I started sliding head first," Comiskey explained years after his first stolen base, "because I figured that to be the most advantageous way of getting a close decision. It is true that as the game developed, the greater number of players went feet first into the bag, but this is risky in more ways than one, even though it is more comfortable than the other. It sometimes means a broken leg, and in any case the runner is unable to see the bag. Of course, combining the phenomenal skill and the extreme speed of a Ty Cobb, the feet first slide has certain advantages, but for all-around efficiency the head slide, in my estimation, has the shade. The runner knows where he is going, he can watch the movements of the fielder and his arms have the edge over the legs in reaching for the bag."

Is the "hook" slide a modern innovation? Comiskey says it is not. As evidence he cites the fact that several of the old Browns used it. Then he calls to mind the Kelly "spread."

"The 'hook slide' is simply physical skill combined with head work," says Comiskey. "As we couldn't depend on substitutes to do either our work or our thinking in the old days we had to figure out certain things for ourselves. The slide was one. I don't think we called it a 'hook,' but it amounted to the same thing. Anyhow, the 'Kelly spread' was as effective and differed little from the hook. Anyone who aspired to be known as a base-runner used it. Among the stars who used it were Welch and Latham of the Browns and Kelly and Williamson of Anson's team.

"Welch slid into a bag either way as, in fact, did most of the crack runners in my day. We only varied the performance as the bruises on our bodies dictated. It was much like broiling a steak. If rare on one side, turn it over. It was before fancy sliding pads had been invented and I want to bear testimony to the fact that the runways were no softer than they are now."

How Comiskey revolutionized the playing around first base, and how the rule makers were compelled to fortify themselves by a new code in order to keep the baseball structure from falling apart, as well as other developments, will be discussed in that portion of the story devoted to the Browns. The traits which he exhibited as a youngster, however, stuck, and if his playing in later years showed any marked difference, it was only in its application to changed conditions. His initiative, dash, quick thinking, grasp of details, inven-

The St. Louis Browns of 1885—the first team ever managed by Comiskey. Players' names, left to right, standing: Strief, McGinnis, O'Neill, Quest, Comiskey, W. Gleason, Nicol; sitting: Wheeler, Latham, Davis, Dolan, Deasley, Lewis.

tiveness and clearness of vision were as conspicuous on the prairies as on the major league diamonds.

The future owner of the White Sox stepped into his first uniform in 1875 but his real baseball education did not begin until 1878, the year he came regularly under the eye of Ted Sullivan. The latter had moved to Dubuque, Iowa, in order to take charge of a news agency, but after he got this into working order his thoughts went to baseball.

Comiskey, being a free lance both as regards baseball and trade,

Sullivan had no trouble in persuading his former school-mate to become a citizen of the Iowa town, the ambitious organizer offering him $50 a month during the summer for playing ball and 20 percent commission for supplying travelers on the Illinois Central Railroad with reading material and confections during his spare time. Combined, this being a considerable advance over the inducements offered by Hogan, master plumber, it was accepted and Comiskey became a "leaguer."

Sullivan, in the intervals needed to check up on his train crews, took time not only to get together the Dubuque team, but also to organize the Northwestern League, the first minor league in the country to finish a season. He had the backing of the late Senator Allison and Congressman D. B. Henderson in this project, the latter at one time speaker of the House of Representatives.

There was no clause in the contract of the 19-year-old player about pitching twice a week or any such modern innovation, but he was expected to prove himself useful at first, second, third and in the outfield, as occasion demanded, besides taking his turn on the mound. The all-around job fitted in with the remark he made later in discussing the Browns when, explaining the dearth of substitutes in that world-famous combination, he said:

"Sometimes we had ten and, occasionally as many as twelve men on the team, but if the manager put a player on the bench in those days, he made an enemy for life."

The team which Sullivan put together in 1878 was a good one but it was greatly improved in '79. Ted then made his first swing around the circuit and picked up Thomas J. Sullivan, a St. Louis boy, who had made good as a catcher with the Worcester team; L. P. Reis, pitcher for the Chicagos the preceding year; W. B. Lapham, first baseman of the Worcesters; Charles Radbourne, of Bloomington, Illinois, a fielder and utility pitcher; while the home talent consisted of William Gleason, third base, and J. Ross, right fielder. Ted himself ranked as infielder and pitcher while Comiskey was pitcher, in- or outfielder, as opportunities presented themselves.

They were no ordinary players, these more or less "unknowns" who broke into the headlines of the Dubuque papers for the first time. Radbourne, for instance, became one of the greatest, if not the premier pitcher of all time; William Gleason added to his fame as short fielder for the Browns; Tom Loftus not only developed into a wonderful second baseman but made an enviable record as manager and owner later in life; Sullivan became the organizer, par excellence, and as for Comiskey, he outshone and outlasted all the rest.

The league, which consisted of Dubuque, Rockford, Omaha and Davenport, brought out many other stars. Rockford had Jack and David Rowe, pitchers; Goodman, first; George Cramer, second; Redmond, short. The incomparable Biddy McPhee played on the Davenport team, while Jim Whitney and W. D. Cantillon, the later to become general manager of the Chicago and Northwestern Railroad, entertained the Omaha fans.

Sullivan's aggregation won the championship but proved a financial failure, and the manager decided that a free lance combination would be less risky, and in 1880 the semi-professional Dubuque Rabbits succeeded the title holders. It would be well to remember these Rabbits, for on this team appeared Charles Comiskey as a regular first baseman, a position which he held for eighteen years. After his pitching arm had begun to give him trouble he had played third base with success but, from the minute he appeared at the initial corner, critics recognized in him a player born to the position.

The royal remuneration of $50 a month failed to turn his head and he continued his railroad run during the winters, his combined duties keeping him in Chicago and Dubuque, by turns, up to the beginning of 1882. During the summer of '81 Sullivan had been invited to bring his "Rabbits" to St. Louis for a game with the newly organized Browns, which he did. The game was played on the Grand Avenue grounds, July 16, and resulted in a 9 to 1 victory for the home team, on which were found "Commy's" old team mates Jack and Bill Gleason.

During the overheated combat St. Louis fans were given the first glimpse of Charles Comiskey, who played an errorless game at first base. The admiration must have been mutual, for from that day to this the "Old Roman" has had nothing but praises for the Mound City, while for years after the old Browns had been swallowed up by the new, they were still naming babies after the great first sacker.

The box score failed to show anything remarkable, but it may be noticed that Tom Loftus got one hit and Comiskey the other, a two-bagger. The lanky visitor also played his position without an error, accepting twelve chances. As they are of historical interest, the statistics of this, his first game in St. Louis, are here given as tabulated in "The National Game":

St. Louis	AB	R	BH	PO	A	E
J. Gleason, 3b	5	1	1	1	3	3
W. Gleason, ss	5	1	1	1	6	0
McCaffery, cf	5	2	2	2	0	0
Seward, c	5	1	3	9	1	1
Morgan, rf	5	1	1	0	1	0
McGinnis, p	5	1	1	0	1	0
Magner, 1f	5	1	1	2	0	0
McDonald, 2b	4	1	0	2	0	0
Gault, 1b	4	0	2	10	0	1
Totals	43	9	12	27	12	5

Dubuque	AB	R	BH	PO	A	E
Sullivan, p, ss	4	1	0	2	4	0
Loftus, 2b	4	0	1	3	3	0

Dubuque	AB	R	BH	PO	A	E
Comiskey, 1b	4	0	1	12	0	0
Ross, c	4	0	0	2	0	0
Burns, 3b	4	0	0	0	2	1
Lear, rf	4	0	0	2	0	0
Morrison, ss, p	4	0	0	0	2	3
Keys, 1f	4	0	0	2	0	0
Phelan, cf	4	0	0	1	0	1
Totals	36	1	2	24	11	5

Earned runs—Browns, 8. Two-base hits—McGinnis, Gault, W. Gleason, Comiskey. Bases on balls—Sullivan and Magner. Umpire—Charles Levis. Official scorer—A.H. Spink.

Although there were others among the visitors more famous than the first baseman, Comiskey seems to have been the cynosure of all eyes and the verdict at the close was that he "would do."

♦ CHAPTER IV ♦

"Der Boss President"

Von der Ahe bursts upon the scene—"Commy" as head of the Browns—"Der boss president" levies fines and is "stung"—Calls Spalding's bluff—The $20,000 train—Comiskey dons brown socks—Never forgets two-bit experiment—Rule makers "fence" him in.

St. Louis was a charter member of the National League and held a franchise in that organization during the years 1876 and 1877. The ambition to possess itself of a winner led to its downfall and the throwing up of the sponge after the close of '77 season. In order to assure a championship to the city the owners signed, among others, Craver, Devlin, Nichols and Hall of the Louisville club. Soon after the signatures of the four had been affixed to contracts, came the revelation of the "throwing" of games in the preceding season by this quartet and their eventual expulsion from organized baseball. The St. Louis management, disgusted by the turn of events, pulled out of the league and the city was not again represented in the parent organization until 1885.

The St. Louis owners were made the victims of circumstances over which they had no control, but the fiasco put baseball out of joint in the Missouri metropolis for a time, and it was not until 1879 that the game began to show signs of life. Then a number of business men and fans combined to organize a team which was christened the Browns.

The elimination of St. Louis from the professional circuit in 1878, as has been recorded, paved the way for a new league and, when the American Association was organized in the winter of 1881, after a western tour of the Athletics of Philadelphia during the preceding summer, the city became a member and remained one for an even decade. During nine of these years Charles A. Comiskey wore the brick-red socks and drew his salary from Christopher Von der Ahe, who was the principal promoter of the Association and the original and only "boss president" of the Browns.

In Von der Ahe the game produced the most unique character that the sport has seen since its formation, and the St. Louis summer garden proprietor is deserving of more than a passing notice before we continue the story of the man who more than anyone else contributed to his sporting and financial success.

Baseball did not originally mean much to Von der Ahe. The waiter in a white apron, who could pick his way with the biggest tray of steins between the round tables under the trees adjacent to the ball park, cut as much figure with him as the mightiest home run clouter on his team. One department of his business was as important as the other as long as the coin jingled in the cash box, but with the onward march of the Browns came a change and Von der Ahe, almost over night, became the most powerful and enthusiastic baseball magnate in the country. The summer garden and grocery store were forgotten as pennant followed pennant on the flag pole.

Borne on the wave of affluence and popularity by the champion Browns he reached the pinnacle of his fame in the period between 1884 and 1889. Having attained the peak the Brotherhood revolt burst, and the fortune he had amassed was dissipated as speedily as it had been accumulated. The friends of his more prosperous days disappeared as the contents of his purse diminished, but it is known to a few that the man to whom he offered a salary of $90 a month in his first baseball venture helped materially to ease his declining days. Of the many who had profited by his largess in the more prosperous days the "Old Roman" was one of the few who stuck to him as a friend to the end. Shortly before he died Chris willed his benefactor the only thing that escaped his creditors—a solid silver statue of a ball player in action, presented to the Browns by Erastus Wyman. This work of the silversmith's art has now an honored place in Comiskey's private office.

Von der Ahe, being too busy in counting and spending the proceeds to give much heed to the game, had the good judgment, early in his career as a baseball magnate, to leave the technical side to others, and from 1884 on it devolved on Comiskey, as captain and manager, to look after the destinies of the Browns, off and on the field.

To outsiders and to the newspaper men Von der Ahe wanted to be known as a real baseball man, a weakness of his which served mostly to furnish the sporting writers with copy for the humorous column. The genius and diplomacy of his manager, and the latter's faculty of acquiescing in everything that Von de Ahe suggested and then doing the opposite, had a tendency to blunt the barbed shafts directed against "der boss president."

Von der Ahe's limited knowledge of the game was never better illustrated than when on a certain occasion he insisted on describing the beauties of his baseball plant to some visiting magnates.

"Some plant, eh?" said the guileless Chris to his visitors as his chest expanded. "I have the biggest diamond in the world, and—"

"Chris, all diamonds are the same size," whispered Comiskey in his ear.

"I mean, gentlemen, the Browns are playing on the biggest infield in the world," promptly corrected the owner.

The dialectic ornaments to Chris's speech have been omitted, as I have yet to hear anyone approximate a real imitation of his inimitable vernacular.

His knowledge of the fine points of the game was as limited as his vocabulary after a losing contest was extensive.

"Them visitors have a punk man in right field," he would inform Comiskey after the heat of the combat was over. "Now, for to-morrow, tell the boys to hit all balls into right."

"Sure, Chris, that was the place to put them, but the boys wouldn't do as I told them" would be the mollifying response of his manager.

"Well, I'll fine every mother's son a month's salary, who double-crosses you, Charlie," would be the comforting assurance of "der boss."

Fining his players was the great indoor sport of Chris. He fined them individually and in platoons. He would sit on the roof of the stand among his directors, and plaster on fines until the pay roll was exhausted.

"Ach, you Gleason, that will cost you a hundred," he would remark as a ball would go scooting through the infield twenty feet from the short stop.

"But, Chris, he wasn't even near the ball," someone would interject.

"But why wasn't he in front of it?" spluttered Chris, and that would wind up that argument.

Arlie Latham, third baseman on the team, who during the late war contributed his bit by coaching Uncle Sam's ball teams in the base camps in England, was always a thorn in the side of Chris. Latham was the clown of the team and was always making life miserable for "der boss." As a consequence he was probably fined oftener than any other member of the team, although Gleason had to share part of the burden. At the many "stated" meetings, which the president insisted on holding in his office there would come a snort from somewhere.

"I don't know who it was, but Gleason, you look guilty and it will cost you a hundred," blustered Chris.

"But, honest, Chris, I never made a sound," pleaded the innocent Bill. "I couldn't, I was just taking a chew."

"Well, maybe it wasn't you, but you are fined fifty for making a pig pen of the office, and," with another outburst from some corner of the room, "the hundred goes for you, Arlie," and the meeting would be adjourned.

The irrepressible Latham having one day violated Von der Ahe's code of ethics was promptly soaked $100. Apparently crestfallen, Arlie, an hour later, met his boss in front of the bar.

"Now, Chris, that fine really doesn't go, does it?" asked the penitent third sacker.

Chris, seeing the contrite expression, admitted it probably had been a little stiff and said he would knock off $50.

"Great," said the player, slapping the president on the back. "I knew you would do that, and Chris, if you will let me have $50 it will make it even."

"Sure," assented Von der Ahe, and Arlie had a new story for the boys in the club house.

"But you are out $50," suggested Comiskey, when the president told how he had remitted part of the fine. This fact having percolated through his cranium, Chris, with a great show of indignation, promised that he would make it $150 next time.

As a matter of fact fines never worried the boys as the majority were always a jump or two ahead when payday came. Should anyone suffer a lapse and have enough money coming to cover the fines the manager usually persuaded Chris to tack on a bonus for some imaginary good piece of work during the month, which would more than cover the penalty.

An even temperament was not characteristic of Chris. It was either sunshine or darkness, with never a trace of twilight in his makeup. It was everything or nothing. He was a gambler by instinct, if not in practice.

A. G. Spalding and A. C. Anson discovered this before the world's series games between the Browns and the White Stockings in 1886.

"Play you winner take all or no series," was the ultimatum from Chicago.

"What do you think about it, Charlie?" asked Chris of his manager.

"Nothing would suit the boys and myself better," answered "Commy."

Comiskey's team won the series, as later related in detail.

In the way of expenses, especially when the outlay promised some return in the spectacular, nothing fazed Von der Ahe in those halcyon days. His great team had proved a gold mine year after year and though he boosted the salary of his manager from $90 a month to $8,000 a year, and some of the other players in proportion, the receipts so far exceeded his expenses that he was hard put to circulate the money. He built a row of apartment houses and named them after his star players. It was surmised by some that when the buildings ceased to be a paying proposition he took a dislike to five of his stars and sold them to make up the difference.

In order to get rid of his surplus cash after the season of 1888, and after "Charlie" had won the fourth successive pennant for him, he decided on a special train from St. Louis to New York, whither he was bound for a world's series with the Giants. He wrote from Cincinnati, where the team was playing, to arrange for it, accommodation to include everything the railroad could offer to his players and guests. The total staggered his secretary, Al Spink, who reported that it would cost $20,000. Chris wired back: "What of it?"

The train was delivered and rolled into New York to the wonder of the natives. Chris paid the bills, railroad as well as hotel, but that was not enough. "Der boss president" wanted to break into print with a new one, so after the second game of the series, which the Browns won, he sent word to each of his players and guests to order a suit of clothes and send the bill to him. He was accommodated and it was figured that the trip to New York cost Von der Ahe approximately $30,000.

It was this type of man with whom Charles Comiskey linked his fortune in 1882, the first year of the American Association—a league which almost entirely centered around Comiskey's four-time champions. Al Spink, among others, had watched the wiry youth at first base at the exhibition games between the Rabbits and the Browns, and during the winter following Spink wrote Comiskey offering the latter a job with the Browns.

"Am I fast enough for that company?" he queried of Sullivan.

"You are too speedy for me," retorted Ted, and "Commy" went.

A year later the player returned the compliment by persuading Von der Ahe to engage Sullivan as manager, pointing out that with Ted as leader there would be only one boss. The prediction came true, and as soon as Chris thought there was room for two, the pair split, which happened towards the fag end of the 1883 season. In the meantime, however, Sullivan had succeeded in getting together a team, which with additions made by Comiskey later, became the wonder of the baseball world.

Calculating his increased earning as sufficient for housekeeping

Comiskey took another important step in 1882, by marrying Miss Nan Kelly, of Dubuque. The two had been engaged for almost three years, but "Commy" wanted to get settled before he led his bride to the altar. It would be a better story were a little baseball romance woven into the first meeting between the two lovers but it must be recorded, for the sake of truth, that there was nothing of the kind. It was only after the newlyweds had moved to St. Louis that Mrs. Comiskey became a fan and a mascot. Years afterwards her husband said:

"I wouldn't know what to do were my wife not to start out with the team on every training trip. She is as much a part of the club as I am and she is the closest pal I ever had."

Two children resulted from the union, one of whom, a boy, died in infancy. The other, Lou, who is known to every fan, is the treasurer of the White Sox Club. He was born in 1885.

Comiskey and Von der Ahe got along famously, even though Chris found it impossible to travel in the same harness with anyone else for any length of time. The reason may be found in the fact that Comiskey never paid the slightest attention to the frequent outbursts of the boss

The Old Roman ready for a hike in the northern woods (1917).

but, penetrating the rough exterior, early discovered a heart as big as that of an ox. On top of this he played the game on the square with Chris, which the latter was quick to acknowledge, and the mercurial magnate boasted to his friends that Charlie never worried him with any tricks, which to the sorely harassed executive meant a lot.

The team which took the field in 1882, with Ed Cuthbert as manager, had some good players in its lineup but it did not compare with those which followed. Before the regular season opened in the spring exhibition games were played, and here is the box score of the first game in which Comiskey appeared in a St. Louis Browns' uniform:

Browns	AB	R	BH	PO	A	E
W. Gleason, ss	5	0	1	0	0	0
Walker, cf	4	0	1	1	0	0
Comiskey, 1b	4	1	1	11	0	0
Davis, 3b	4	1	1	1	0	2
Smiley, 2b	4	0	0	1	3	0
Seward, c	4	0	0	13	0	3
McGinnis, p	4	0	0	0	2	1
Cuthbert, lf	4	0	2	0	0	1
Shappert, rf	4	0	1	0	0	0
Totals	37	2	7	27	5	7

Standards	AB	R	BH	PO	A	E
Morgan, 3b	4	1	1	2	0	0
Simpson, 2b	4	1	0	2	0	0
Decker, cf	4	1	1	2	1	3
Cunningham, lf	4	0	0	8	1	0
Wagner, ss	4	0	2	3	4	0
Croft, 1b	3	0	0	5	2	0
Hogan, p	3	0	0	1	10	0
Dillon, rf	3	1	1	1	0	0
Houtz, c	3	0	0	3	0	0
Totals	32	4	5	27	18	3

Innings	1	2	3	4	5	6	7	8	9
Browns	2	0	0	0	0	0	0	0	0—2
Standards	1	0	2	0	0	0	0	1	0—4

Total bases—Browns, 8; Standards, 3. Umpire—Dave Ring. Time, 1:35.

Comiskey's first appearance against the Browns, like his first game with them, was a defeat, but the rough spots had been smoothed a week later and the Browns walloped the life out of the Standards.

The American Association made its big organizing campaign on the platform of 25-cent ball, instead of 50 cents, which was charged in the National League. The price cutting, although popular in St. Louis, proved a mistake from a financial viewpoint elsewhere, but the venture was a bonanza for Von der Ahe almost from the start, and the following year Ted Sullivan was given the task of organizing a winner.

The two-bit experiment in 1882 was not forgotten by Comiskey, and when he came to Chicago and was taken to task by his fellow magnates for his encouragement of 25-cent ball, he replied that as long as he controlled his own team the bleacher patrons would have an equal show with the grand stand spectators. Consequently the "uncovered" accommodations at the South Side Park in Chicago approximate 25 percent of the whole—by far the largest in the league.

"It doesn't bring in quite as much money at the gate as the more expensive seats but it gives a greater number a chance to see my team and that is the big thing with me," Comiskey said in answer to the criticism.

The team which Sullivan handed to Von der Ahe for the 1883 season, after the Browns had finished fifth in a six-club league in 1882, consisted of the following:

Tom Deasley, Tom Dolan and Tom Sullivan, catchers; Tony

Mullane, Charles Hodnett, George McGinnis and Henry Oberbeck, pitchers; Charles Comiskey, first base; George Strief, second base; Walter A. Latham, third base; William Gleason, short stop; Eddie Cuthbert, left field; Oberbeck or Mullane, center field; Hugh Nicol, right field.

Sullivan, as manager, parted company with Von de Ahe before the season was over and in the following year took over the management of the St. Louis Union League club, which only lasted out the season.

Jimmy Williams succeeded Ted Sullivan and hung on until the middle of the 1884 season, when, after another one of his outbursts, Chris found himself without a leader. In this dilemma Von der Ahe turned to the twenty-five-year-old youngster from Chicago, who was still lean and possibly inexperienced, but with a head full of new ideas as to how the game should be played. It was a leap in the dark for the first sacker, but he promised Chris that he would try, and from that day to the winter of 1901 he held the managerial reins.

The Browns of 1883 had come within one game of landing the pennant, and now with Comiskey in full charge things began to hum, although, perhaps due to a bad start, the team was unable to do better than fourth in a twelve club league. The team finished 74 points behind the champion Metropolitans of New York. It was made up of the following players:

Tom Deasley and Tom Dolan, catchers; William Widmer and George McGinnis, pitchers; Charles Comiskey, first base; George Strief and Joe Quest, second; Walter A. Latham, third; William Gleason, short stop; J. E. (Tip) O'Neill, left field; Fred Lewis and Harry Wheeler, center; Hugh Nicol, right.

Comiskey had, at the start of his league career, shown a number of new wrinkles to American Association fans. Up to his advent it had been the custom of the first baseman to glue himself to the bag. Comiskey cut loose from the sack, edging out in the territory towards right field. He taught the pitcher how to cover first base in an emergency, although he was one of the few basemen who relieved the twirler of much of this work. The innovation did not look natural to many of the old timers, but in a comparatively short time every first sacker had moved out. Comiskey's next logical move was to shift the whole infield, in or out, as occasions demanded.

The pastime began to have a new meaning to the fans with the disappearance of the motionless first baseman and with the mobile infield. The Browns were hailed as missionaries of a new game and they soon had the reputation of being the speediest combination in the country. Given speed, pitching and head work Comiskey figured he had the world beaten. He went along on this theory and won four championships in a row.

Batting was not underrated but, although he had his share of sluggers on the Browns, Comiskey did not consider stick work the most important feature except as it synchronized with other departments of the game. Years later—in 1906—this was again demonstrated when the White Sox, the "hitless wonders," won the World's Championship after having captured the American League pennant on a minimum of batting.

Comiskey himself was not a heavy hitter but he had a knack of worrying the pitcher and his .250 or .275 batting average for the season meant more to his team than the ordinary .300 percentage. When once on the bases the troubles of the opponents began. Never a trick escaped him and he rapidly became a terror as a base runner. That he stole 62 bases in 1887 and 77 in 1888 showed how well he could control his feet.

The leader of the Browns was speedy but he was far from being a Sheffield Handicap man. There were many who could beat him in a sprint, but few who could get more out of base-running than he.

Given an even break in sliding into a base, nine times out of ten he gained the decision, the fielders usually making a stab at the shadow instead of the substance, and this despite the fact that they had a mark of over six feet to aim at.

Below is shown Comiskey's batting and fielding records for the time he served in the major leagues, "pinch hitting" giving him a slightly higher total in the number of games played as a batter.

BATTING

Year, Club and League.	Games	Hits	Runs	Avg.
1882—St. Louis A. A.	78	71	66	.244
1883—St. Louis A. A.	91	99	67	.264
1884—St. Louis A. A.	99	102	42	.257
1885—St. Louis A. A.	83	89	58	.260
1886—St. Louis A. A.	131	149	94	.260
1887—St. Louis A. A.	128	218	111	.368
1888—St. Louis A. A.	137	156	104	.271
1889—St. Louis A. A.	139	169	105	.288
1890—Chicago P. L.	88	93	53	.248
1891—St. Louis A. A.	135	144	83	.257
1892—Cincinnati N. L.	140	124	60	.223
1893—Cincinnati N. L.	62	58	31	.225
1894—Cincinnati N. L.	59	61	26	.265
Totals for 13 years	1,370	1,533	900	.264

FIELDING

Year, Club and League.	Games	Putouts	Assists	Errors	Avg.
1882—St. Louis A. A.	77	869	18	29	.976
1883—St. Louis A. A.	91	940	47	32	.968
1884—St. Louis A. A.	99	974	36	35	.966
1885—St. Louis A. A.	82	861	31	20	.970
1886—St. Louis A. A.	123	1,152	44	29	.976
1887—St. Louis A. A.	120	1,214	40	30	.975
1888—St. Louis A. A.	133	1,379	41	38	.972
1889—St. Louis A. A.	134	1,233	39	32	.973
1890—Chicago P. L.	88	882	45	22	.968
1891—St. Louis A. A.	130	1,311	40	37	.970

Year, Club and League.	Games	Putouts	Assists	Errors	Avg.
1892—Cincinnati N. L.	140	1,460	71	25	.983
1893—Cincinnati N. L.	62	671	21	14	.980
1894—Cincinnati N. L.	59	558	26	16	.978
Totals for 13 years	1,338	13,504	499	359	.973

From the figures it will be seen that he batted above the .300 mark but once in his major league career—1887—when he finished the season with an average of .368. In fielding he reached .983 in his first year at Cincinnati, where he played in every one of the 140 games scheduled.

Comiskey's career as a player, captain, manager and owner is shown at a glance by the following table:

1875–1898	Player—pitcher and fielder.
1883–89	Captain and first baseman of the St. Louis Browns.
1884–89	Manager of the St. Louis Browns.
1890	Captain and manager of the Chicago Brotherhood team.
1891	Captain and manager St. Louis Browns.
1892–94	Manager Cincinnati National League team.
1895–99	Owner and manager St. Paul Western League team.
1900	Owner and manager Chicago White Sox.
1901–	Owner Chicago White Sox.

The new ideas advanced by Comiskey have been frequently exploited by chroniclers from the time he began, but little has been recorded about the flaws he discovered. Bill Gleason, his teammate, thinks he was responsible for half the changes in playing methods. Among others he is held responsible for the coaching box and the double umpire system. James A. Hart, former president of the Cubs, related to the writer several years ago the reason for the barriers at first and third:

"The chalk lines which enclose the coaching boxes were added to the field diagram after Charles Comiskey had demonstrated their necessity," he said. "Comiskey and Bill Gleason used to plant themselves on each side of the visiting catcher and comment on his breeding, personal habits, skill as a receiver, or rather lack of it, until the unlucky backstop was unable to tell whether one or half a dozen balls were coming his way. Not infrequently the umpire came in for a few remarks.

"'He's a sweet bird, isn't he, Bill?' Comiskey would chirp.

"'Never heard of him before, did you, Commy?' would be the dulcet reply of Gleason.

"'The cat must have brought him in and put him in the keeping of the umpire or else how could he last more than an inning?' and so to the end of the chapter.

"This solicitous attention did not add to the efficiency of the backstop, so for the sake of not unduly increasing the population of the insane asylums or encouraging justifiable homicide, the coacher's box was invented. This helped out the catcher, but the pitcher and other players on the opposing team, were still at the mercy of Comiskey, and I know of no man who had a sharper tongue, who was in command of more biting sarcasm, or who was quicker at repartee."

Comiskey's "deadly" coaching centered in the fact that he was playing the game every minute. After a contest had been lost he could stretch and forget it, but he never permitted anyone to lose sight of the fact that he was on the field to win. In later years he carried a similar spirit with him to the grand stand, and as for the bench—old timers recount with glee his antics in the "coop."

"If I could find the time I would wish for no better vacation than to travel with Comiskey and sit with him on the bench," said the late John T. Brush. "If I also could have a shorthand writer with me I would be fixed for entertainment for the winter. No man could put more in a sentence than Charles Comiskey."

His nervousness on the bench was often taken advantage of by his men. It was usually his habit to unconsciously glide from one end of the bench to the other during a game, or even during an inning. Frank Isbell, who aided materially in winning the first World's Championship for the White Sox, and who originally broke into the game with Comiskey in the Western League, is credited with having driven a nail from the underside of the board at St. Paul. The point was elevated just high enough to become rasping without being conspicuous, although the rest of the players were "next."

The fact that Comiskey was in civilian clothes added to the zest of the undertaking. In due time came the tight inning and the rapid shifting of the boss. The hit that tied it up produced unwonted action. Commy slid over the obstruction but he did not discover until after the game was over that his trousers were bifurcated laterally as well as longitudinally.

♦ Chapter V ♦

A $15,000 Slide

Comiskey starts organizing his four-time winners—Establishes a monopoly in pennants—Praise for Ted Sullivan—He never forgets—Browns and Anson's White Stockings compared—How "Commy's" first world's title was won—Broadway lights Browns' undoing.

Pretzels and ball players, being of equal importance to Von der Ahe, it devolved on his manager to organize for the campaigns which culminated in Curt Welch's $15,000 slide and a world's championship in '86. Comiskey started out by adding William Widmer to his 1884 pitching staff, Joe Quest to his infield, Fred Lewis, Harry Wheeler and the greatest of sluggers, Tip O'Neill, to his outfield. Those discarded were Tom Sullivan, Tony Mullane, Charles Hodnett, Henry Oberbeck and Eddie Cuthbert.

Before the season was over Comiskey discovered that he did not have a real pennant contender and during the winter came the final rounding out of the "four-time winners," the pride of Missouri. Here they are:

Caruthers and Foutz, pitchers; Bushong, catcher; Comiskey, first base; Robinson, second base; Latham, third base; Gleason, short stop; O'Neill, left field; Welch, center field; Nicol, right field.

This was the regular lineup of the Browns. A few utility players figured during succeeding years but the team was known as a ten-man combination, and the changes for three seasons were inconsequential. Hudson was added to the pitching staff in 1886, while "Silver" King and Boyle were signed in 1887.

Von der Ahe's brainstorm wrecked the wonderful combination during the winter of 1887, Foutz, Caruthers and Bushong being sold to the Brooklyn American Association team and Bill Gleason and Curt Welch to the Philadelphia Athletics.

Nothing brought out Comiskey's genius for leadership as the campaign of 1888, and it is doubtful if such a feat has ever been equaled in the annals of baseball as he performed that year. Five of his greatest players—over one-half of his regular lineup—had been transferred to other teams in his own league.

Few of the baseball wiseacres expected the Browns to do much better than last, and Von der Ahe, from having been one of the most popular men in St. Louis, found it convenient to keep out of the sight of the enraged followers of the champions.

Despite the terrific handicap Comiskey did his best to mollify the fans, although his friends tried to persuade him to sever his connection with Von der Ahe. He started out at a fair pace and finished the season like a whirlwind, in first place, with this team:

King, Hudson, Chamberlin and Devlin, pitchers; Boyle and Milligan, catchers; Comiskey, first base; Robinson, second; Latham, third; White, short stop; O'Neill, left field; Lyons, center; McCarthy, right.

Brooklyn, which had profited by the trade for Foutz, Caruthers and Bushong, finished in second place, 52 points behind the winners, while the Athletics, who had been strengthened by the acquisition of Gleason and Welch, beat out Cincinnati for third place.

The next year the race simmered down to a contest between the Browns and Brooklyn, into which the personal element largely entered. Toward the close of the season two games, forfeited by the Browns to Brooklyn, came near breaking up the league, as the Board of Directors in a special meeting upheld the action of Comiskey in withdrawing from the field in one game and refusing to take his chances against the Flatbush rowdies on the Sabbath, in another. Brooklyn won but the Browns were behind only two games at the finish with this team:

Jack Boyle and John Milligan, catchers; Jack Stivetts and Silver King, pitchers; Comiskey, first base; William Robinson, second; W. (Shorty) Fuller, short stop; Arlie Latham, third; Tip O'Neill, left field; Eddie Duffie, center; Tommy McCarthy, right; Henry Lyons, utility outfielder.

With the end of the '89 season Comiskey's career in St. Louis practically came to a close, although he returned in 1891, after the Brotherhood war, for one season. The final drive for an Association pennant saw the Browns in second place—as low, with one exception, as Comiskey ever fell in the Association while manager. His nature, though, rebelled against figuring worse than first. It was while a number of his friends congratulated him over the fact that the White Sox had finished as well as second in 1916 the "Old Roman" gave voice to this aphorism:

"First place is the only subject of conversation. Everybody chokes up before they get as far as second."

After Boston had been awarded the pennant it was curtains for the American Association. It had so fallen upon evil days that its demise was almost painless, except to those who were unfortunate enough to hold the bag. The National League, as a twelve-club organization, swallowed up some of the Association franchises. Among the new members in the parent body was Chris Von der Ahe, who stuck as "der boss president" until 1898. History has dealt fairly with both owner and manager but it is doubtful if the name of Chris Von

Charles A. Comiskey (left) and A. G. Spalding snapped together for the first and only time. This meeting took place at Comiskey Park just before the famous White Sox–Giants world tour.

der Ahe ever would have figured in major league baseball if he had had any other leader for his team than Charles Comiskey. Without the latter there probably would have been no championships and with no title holders to draw the fans, there could have been no chance for "der boss" to make a splurge.

Comiskey has never been loquacious in discussing the responsibility for getting the Browns together except to credit Ted Sullivan with the major part of it. He permitted Von der Ahe to share in the honors, although it is well known that the functions of the latter consisted in supplying the cash, which others had earned for him.

As a matter of fact Von der Ahe received more for players than he paid although his liberality with the men personally often swung the scales in Comiskey's favor.

It was a good team which Sullivan put together in 1883, but for the sake of the reputation of others it should be pointed out that it was not the combination which won the title for St. Louis later on. Some few cogs were missing at the start. Robinson, Welch, O'Neill, Bushong, Caruthers and Foutz were not on hand when Comiskey took the reins in 1884. Comiskey dismisses the subject with the remark:

"I think Ted found most of them."

Sullivan admits that he did some scouting for the Browns after he quit as manager but the fact remains that it was up to Comiskey to pass on them regardless of who picked them out. What was even more important, it was up to him to mold them into that frictionless machine which steam-rolled its way to four pennants.

As far as the playing end was concerned there was only one boss during the seven out of nine years and Comiskey was "it." The campaigns—league, world's or merely exhibition tours—were all thought out by him. He never went to bed without figuring out a plan of strategy for the following day and he held himself responsible for the smallest detail, off and on the field. In this his marvelous memory stood him in good stead. Once heard, a thing was never forgotten. It is deemed appropriate to digress for an excursion into this phase of his personality.

I have rubbed elbows with people in most corners of the globe but I have yet to meet a human being with the retentive memory of Comiskey. Repeated demonstrations of that faculty have been to me a constant source of wonderment for many years.

Going through Memphis once on a spring trip with the White Sox a stranger boarded the train, inquiring for Mr. Comiskey. I directed him towards the owner's stateroom, but on our way down the aisle of the car we met the "Old Roman."

Not being endowed with "Commy's" gift, I have forgotten the names of the characters which figured in this little morning drama, but at any rate the visitor and, we will call him Jim, made a courtly bow, at the same time expressing his pleasure at seeing the owner of the White Sox.

"I was one of your admirers in the days of the old Browns," he explained, "and hearing that you were to pass through, I came down to shake hands with you and wish you all the luck in the world for the coming season."

Comiskey regarded the lanky caller for just a moment, then reached out his hand.

"Well, Jim, how are you and how is Mrs. _____, and, I suppose John and Mary have grown up and are married by this time."

Having elaborated on the condition of the family tree Jim departed and the train moved on.

"An old friend of yours?" I enquired.

"Sure, but for a moment I was embarrassed, not being able to recall his name," came the answer. "I didn't know his family very well as I never met them but once."

There was an interval of twenty-two years between the meetings.

This faculty came into daily use on the ball field and it explained many of the phenomenal feats exhibited by this master of the craft. Once he had spotted a weak point in an opposing player he never forgot it though he might not have occasion to put it to a test for years. Thus it happened that an enthusiastic scout rushed into the presence of Owner Comiskey with the tale of a marvelous find.

"But he can't play the sun field."

"How do you know?" came the query.

"I saw him try it once," and the deal was off.

The ivory hunter then discovered that Comiskey had seen the player in action several years before on one of the spring exhibition trips but he had never forgotten the man's failings.

It was so during his playing days. A new opponent would plant himself at the plate, backed by a big bat and a reputation as a slugger. A signal from first base to the pitcher and the newcomer would whiff on three high ones close to the breast bone.

"How did you know what he was weak on, Commy?" the puzzled Caruthers asked.

"Why, didn't I see him put a ball over the fence on a low one on the outside a few years ago up around Galena? I figured he didn't like the insiders."

It was the same all the way down the line. Once a move was mirrored in "Commy's" mind he never lost it. Combine this with clear judgment, the faculty of meeting emergencies on the instant, without showing a trace of the "rattles," and is it any wonder that championships have trailed the "Old Roman" through nearly four decades?

Many critics have insisted that, player for player, the old Browns did not measure up to Anson's heroic legion of 1885 and '86. Perhaps they did not, but glance at the result of the two series between the teams of Comiskey and Anson. Anson's own opinion of his team is best given in his book, "A Ball Player's Career," and this is, in part, what he says:

> The team that brought the pennant back to Chicago in the year of 1885 and 1886 was, in my estimation, not only the strongest team that I ever had under my management but, taken all in all, one of the strongest teams that has ever been gotten together in the history of the [National] League, the position of left field, which was still being played by Dalrymple, being

> its only weak spot. * * * In its pitching department it was second in strength to none of its competitors and behind the bat were Flint and Kelly, both of whom were widely and favorably known.
>
> The outfield was, to say the least, equal to that of any other of the league clubs, and the infield admittedly the strongest in the country. This was the infield that became famous as "Chicago's stone wall," that name being given to it for the reasons that the only way that a ball could be gotten through it was to bat it so high that it was out of reach.

In order to refresh the memory of the reader it might be well to recall that on this great team Larry Corcoran, John Clarkson, James McCormick and John Flynn were the pitchers; Mike Kelly and Frank Flint, catchers; A. C. Anson, Fred Pfeffer, Ed Williamson and Tom Burns, made up the infield while Abner Dalrymple, George Gore, Jimmy Ryan and Billy Sunday and others cavorted in the outfield.

The best that this famous aggregation could get was a draw with the Browns in '85, being decisively beaten in '86. Physically, perhaps, Anson's legion may have outclassed the Browns. If they did, what about the 1882 White Stockings, which Mike Kelly dubbed the greatest team of all time? They were great, in Kelly's opinion, mainly on account of the size of the players, whose heroic proportions were enough to inspire fear in their opponents the minute they marched across the field. Yet, regardless of a difference of opinion Anson's Eighty-sixers could be put down as "some" team.

It was recognized that in Clarkson and Kelly, Anson had one of the best batteries that ever swapped signals. He himself was a fine first sacker and a mighty slugger. Then size up the rest and permit them to mill around Ed Williamson, in Anson's estimation the greatest player that ever lived. Quite a bunch that, and yet they were beaten when it came to a test.

In batting strength the White Stockings surpassed the Browns. In fielding there was not much to choose, although, if there were an edge, Chicago had it. In pitchers there were Caruthers, Foutz and Hudson, against the redoubtable Clarkson and McCormick, while as a receiver Bushong had to practically hold his own against the veterans Kelly and Flint. Then what decided? We hazard the opinion that strategy did it. Anson explains the 1886 series like this:

"We were beaten, and fairly beaten, but had some of the players taken as good care of themselves prior to these games as they were in the habit of doing when the league season was in full swing, I am inclined to believe that there might have been a different tale to tell."

Here is another comment on the Browns by the leader of the Chicago team:

"The St. Louis Browns was a strong organization, a very strong one, and when we met them in a series of games for what was styled at the time the world's championship, in the fall of 1885, they would have been able, in my estimation, to have given any and all of the [National] League clubs a race for the money."

The 1885 series had been a see-saw affair with the base hits scattered between the Alleghanies and the Mississippi River. The first game, which was played in Chicago, was a tie. Of the next three at St. Louis, Chicago took one and the Browns two. Then followed a contest at Pittsburgh, which was forfeited to Chicago in six innings. The followers of the Browns always claimed that it was a species of robbery. Of the two games at Cincinnati, which closed the series, each took one, the final result being three apiece with one drawn.

As has already been mentioned, Spalding's and Anson's suggestion for the 1886 series, of the "winner to take all" was eagerly snapped up by Comiskey. Chicago took the first tilt at home, but after this game they rapidly faded, but the bitterness exhibited set a record for world's series games. It was the best four out of seven and history insists that the series was decided on a wild pitch by Clarkson. Such is not in accordance with the facts, although its proponents may prove their point through the elastic interpretation of what constitutes a wild heave. Comiskey was there, he was partially responsible for the run, and got the ball that Clarkson pitched, so he should know. He dictated this:

> The score stood a tie at 3 to 3 in the tenth inning with Curt Welch on third. His own single, an error and an out had put him on the far corner. In order to worry Clarkson, who was pitching, Welch took a long lead off third, too long in fact, for which I was partially responsible as I was coaching. On the first ball pitched Welch was so far away from the bag that Mike Kelly, who was catching, could have nailed him easily. Bushong had let it go by without offering to swing at it.
>
> It was then that Welch showed his usual brainwork. Curt figured that if he kept at the same risky distance from the bag Kelly would signal for a high ball on the inside in order to have the advantage of a quick throw to Burns. It turned out just like that. Clarkson burned one by Bushong's shirt and Kelly in his eagerness to get the ball away to catch Welch slightly fumbled it and it rolled about ten feet. Welch must have divined the fumble, for he was off like a flash towards the plate. Never in my life, I believe, have I seen a man go as fast. He seemed to skim over the ground.
>
> No one knew better than Kelly what that run would mean. Over $15,000 hinged on it. If Welch made it, it would probably be the day coach for many of the White Stockings as they had backed themselves well if not wisely. If Kelly could get the ball on him Chicago still had a chance, not only at the game but at the series. If he lost the race, all was over, as it would make the fourth win for us.
>
> As it actually happened Kelly never had a chance, either to

> get the man or the ball. As Welch slid into the plate I pounced on the ball. Kelly was reaching for it, but I beat him to it, as I was right on the heels of Curt. That ball is still in my possession, plated and boxed.

An interval of just twenty years was to elapse before Comiskey would annex another world's title. In the following year, after another pennant had been flung to the breeze, the world's series, through the insistence of the fans in different parts of the country, and with the ready acquiescence of Von der Ahe, became a barn storming tour, Detroit winning after the teams had exhibited in Pittsburgh, Brooklyn, New York, Philadelphia, Boston, Washington, Baltimore and Chicago, besides their own home towns. The series earned more coin than glory that fall.

In 1888, with the fourth and last title for St. Louis, the Browns were beaten by the New York Giants in a memorable series, six games to four, the pitching of Tim Keefe for the Giants being the feature, this sterling hurler winning every start and he pitched four out of the ten games.

Von der Ahe's "special," with the attendant embellishments, probably had something to do with the defeat as even the strict disciplinary measures of the manager failed to keep the boys in check as long as the president insisted on paying all the bills, regardless of what was ordered from the menu.

♦ CHAPTER VI ♦

Coming of the Supermen

Giants of former days—Comiskey's own story of the Browns—Explains why they won four pennants—Hard to keep them on the bench—"Kid" Gleason's reminiscences of the "Old Roman"—Others pass judgment on "Commy."

The era in which the Browns figured was a period equally divided between romance and cold-blooded deals. Men cheerfully went broke for an ideal while others did everything but commit murder for the sake of a dollar. It was the luck of the game that the ideal predominated and thus the sportsmanlike development of baseball overshadowed the financial. After the Civil War decade the game, like the country as a whole, was largely in the making for a few years. Shift followed shift, rules were changed overnight, and the sport generally took on a new complexion. Then, as it happened—and who shall explain it?—a race of supermen came to the front in baseball. Brawn and muscle were combined with gray matter to an extent unknown in these latter days. Genius and the slugger worked hand in hand in perfecting the pastime so that little was left to the highly mechanical artists of today.

The type of men engaged made it a red-blooded sport, and less time was spent in sizing up the "house" and figuring on next year's contract than is the case these days. It was a knockdown and drag-out on the field with few holds barred. No one asked for quarter and the game was never lost until the last man was out. A split finger, a lacerated leg or even a broken bone was not considered a passport to the hospital. Nothing short of crutches kept a man out of his position and marriage or death alone were considered of sufficient importance to warrant absence from the field.

It is not the intention to single out the Browns and their leader to represent all that was great baseball in those days, as there were other giants abroad, but the St. Louis combination will, at least, serve as the main text. In the Hall of Fame which contained the old Chicago White Stockings, the famed Detroits, the Providence Grays, the herculean New Yorks and others of little less renown, the Browns size up pretty well. Comiskey, who has managed many a team since the days of the four-time winners, finds an actual comparison with modern teams more or less an impossibility, mainly due to the difference in rules. He dictated the following:

> I would not be on the level did I not confess that I always have believed that the old Browns were a great team, one of the greatest ever organized. In brains and punch they would measure up to the standard of any team today, both individually and as a combination, but there is no possible way to judge their effectiveness on a diamond today under modern rules.
>
> Before the Browns went out of existence the rules were perfected as they are found to-day but during the greater part of their existence the game was conducted under a code that radically differed from the modern style of play. The principal changes centered around the pitcher and there is no way of proving how Radbourne, Sweeney, Foutz, Caruthers, Spalding and others would have behaved at the present distance and under the restrictions which govern the pitcher of to-day. Nor

is it possible to judge how the Cicottes, Johnsons, Alexanders and Ruths would have fared had they been compelled to pitch instead of throwing or had they been permitted to employ the hop, step and jump, for instance.

It is true that many of the star pitchers, under the old rules, overlapped into the next era, but it is not on record that any of the old-timers shone to any great extent. Many have argued that this proved conclusively that the twirlers of the Eighties were not as effective as those of the Nineties. Not at all. The effectiveness was lost, partly because they had seen their best days and partly because it is hard for an old dog to learn new tricks.

I had some great pitchers while in St. Louis. At first they only "pitched" the ball fifty feet. They had an allowance of six bases on balls which was neutralized to some extent by four strikes. Later on the "throw" became a free-for-all, overhand or any style the pitcher chose. With the change in the throw also came the added freedom in the box and a hop, step and jump was in order in 1886 with the pitcher's box seven feet long and four feet wide. Originally the pitcher was handicapped by the privilege of the batsman in calling for a "high" or a "low" ball and no one to-day has any idea what that meant. In 1887 the pitcher was chained down practically to what he is today except as to distance which was not lengthened until 1893. The four strike rule was changed back to three in 1888. Giving the batter a hit when he was sent to first on bases on balls was also done away with.

Taking into consideration the different conditions which prevailed then it would not be fair actually to compare players of thirty and forty years ago with those of to-day. The human element alone should figure and taking this into consideration I do not have to apologize for the old Browns. They were composed of the greatest bunch of fighters which were ever brought together, and as for gameness they were surpassed by none.

It might be mentioned that our real lineup during the most successful seasons was boiled down to ten or eleven men. Minor hurts were never taken into consideration and it would have to be broken bones to keep anyone out. As everybody on the team wanted to be in the game every day I had to use some diplomacy in getting the extra man or two to stick to the bench now and then. The pitcher who hurled an extra inning game one day would feel aggrieved if he did not get a chance to repeat or to play in the outfield the following day.

Such was the spirit of the men and in that lay the secret of the four championships. I would not seem to underrate the technical skill of such men as Gleason, Welch, Foutz, Caruthers, Bushong, Nichol, Hudson, Latham, O'Neill, Robinson and others of those who were with me. They were wonderful players and trained under modern conditions would shine on any field. There was not a slow thinker in the lot, in fact it took some speed to keep up with the bunch in this department.

The team from 1884 to the close of 1887 had everything needed. It had speed on the bases and in the field; it had enough sluggers to balance artistic fielding and before it was broken up its team work was second to none in the United States. It was not overburdened with signals, as every member was expected to know just what to do in an emergency. The team at the start of the Association played a different style of game from most others. I have been given a certain amount of credit for this, but regardless of that the team never was tied down by precedent. It constantly blasted its way along new roads and thus we got the credit for being original.

One of our strong points might be called the "open" game. The players were pulled "in" or "out" as occasion demanded and again we were praised for making the game spectacular. No one to-day would notice such departure as it would be considered part of the game. The pastime, however, was in the making and that is why the Browns cut such a large swath. They were always trying, not only to keep abreast of the times, but to keep a step or two ahead, and this conferred on us progressiveness. No player on the team was ever taken in by the same trick a second time and he would be considered dull were he not to improve upon it, to the disadvantage of him who originally played it on him. Every player simply had to keep his wits about him, for if he did not the guying to which he would be subjected would tend to wise him up.

There were "boners" pulled by players in my younger days, but I hardly think that they were as glaring as to-day. The disgrace was felt more keenly then than seems to be the case at present. We didn't seem to be able to stand the kidding which followed a mistake as well as they do now. Perhaps we were more thin-skinned and thus saw to it that we didn't repeat.

Our record, especially in fielding, did not look as artistic as that of some other combinations, but that was because no one was afraid to take chances. No one cared for errors, not if he knew that he attempted to make the play the right way. It was only when he shirked the ball that his teammates started to "ride" him, and I want to testify to the effectiveness of their "riding." They were wonders at it.

Looking back over the statistics I believe, though, that the record in fielding was pretty good after our machine got to going. Robinson at second was as shifty as anyone in those days, Gleason at short was a wonder and Latham, although not the greatest third baseman in the world, was no slouch at playing the position, and he was valuable in many other ways, especially base running. The fans seemed to think that I did well enough at first.

In the outfield I had one of the greatest of all fly chasers and base runners in Curt Welch, and one of the greatest sluggers in the history of the game in Tip O'Neill. In 1887, I believe it was, he hit for an average of .492, the biggest percentage ever rung up in the major leagues, but it must be taken into consideration that in that year bases on balls counted as hits. Still when walks were not profitable Tip was there with the bat.

Hugh Nicol, Foutz and Caruthers took turns in the outfield and were all handy men, but one of the most valuable on the team was Bushong, behind the bat. There was one of the gamest catchers I ever saw, one who never knew when he was beaten, or hurt either, for that matter. Taking into account our base running, Welch's especially, and Bushong's throwing we always could worry the opposition both offensively and defensively.

The men I have mentioned were with me early in my career. Later on came Hudson, King, Chamberlin and Stivetts as pitchers; Boyle and Milligan, catchers, and the speedy McCarthy as an outfielder. I had other shifty players towards the close, but none who measured up to the original Browns.

I have been asked many times to compare the Browns and Anson's White Stockings of '85 and '86. Comparisons being odious I hesitate to go into details. Anson had a great team, one of the best I have ever seen. He had men of brains and originality in that outfit, men who could field and hit the ball with the best in the land. In Clarkson and Kelly he had one of the greatest batteries of all times, and Anson himself had demonstrated his right to lead the team.

I also commanded a good team, I would even call it great, but perhaps, with not quite as many outstanding stars as in the Chicago aggregation. We met in '85 and it was a draw—a good many of the St. Louis fans regarded it as a victory for us. Again we clashed in 1886 and the Browns won decisively. Anson in his own book has passed judgment on his own team. I shall let the series of 4 to 2 speak for mine.

Comiskey, it might be noticed, didn't say much of his own connection in discussing the Browns.

Those who played with him or under him are not so chary. Bill Gleason, the original "Kid," is one of the latter. When he heard that

I contemplated writing the life story of "Commy" he sent me the following and I give it as he wrote it:

> I am much pleased to hear you are writing a story about Comiskey as I have often thought something of the kind would be very interesting to his many admirers. He and I were close friends in our younger days. Of course now our paths lie far apart but for nine years while we were with the Browns we roomed together, both in hotels and on the sleeping cars, and I have never found a friend since whom I could so love and respect.
>
> "Commy" was kind, generous and considerate and a *winner*. He never went to sleep at night until he had figured out how he was going to win the game the next day. As a player I consider him the best first baseman of his day, quick to judge and almost quicker to act. He played a deep first base and, covering much territory, the runners were kept busy watching him. He was great at holding the runner at first and the pitcher was saved a great deal of work, as, with "Commy" on the bag, he seldom had to leave the box.
>
> I don't know if it is known that "Commy" was the means of the umpire judging the game from behind the pitcher. This happened at Cincinnati with Bob Ferguson umpiring. He and Comiskey had an argument, Charlie claiming that the "ump" didn't see the play or else that he gave the Browns the worst of the decision. Ferguson, in a temper, went behind the pitcher, and, of course, could see all the bases better from there. From that experiment grew the double umpire system.
>
> Even as a young man he was a first class manager. Here is an illustration. In 1884 we were scheduled to play an exhibition game in New Haven. Robinson, the second baseman, failed to report, and "Commy" had only eight men (they didn't carry a coach-full of players then). He scoured the town for a player to fill out, and finally got an amateur whom he put into right field.

> He picked the right one, as the stranger was the means of winning the game in the ninth inning by catching a fly ball with two men gone, and it was a tough one at that.
>
> Comiskey was the first man I ever saw who slid head first to a base. He was a hard worker and always set his men an example of good team work, making sacrifice plays and doing everything to win, but never thinking of himself. He also knew how to take a joke, as the following incident will show.
>
> During the season of 1888, while playing against the Brooklyns, we had our uniforms drying at a sporting club called the Athletics. During the night some members distributed about a bushel of red pepper, filling our knickers and shoes. They donated about half a pound to "Commy" and after once on the field we only touched the high spots. The weather was beastly warm, which contributed to the speed of the Brownies, who were up in the air most of the time, but we got even by winning the game, 3 to 2. "Commy" took the whole thing good-naturedly, probably secretly rejoicing at the pep displayed by the players.
>
> There was always good discipline among the Browns, but occasionally some of the boys would take advantage of the manager. Comiskey was particular about the boys being in bed early but occasionally they played hookey. Robinson, for instance, would ostentatiously take his key from the rack and retire only to slide down the fire escape. It was a lively bunch with which "Commy" had to contend, but they all liked him and loved him as a brother, as he was on the square with everybody.

Others of Comiskey's friends have contributed their appreciation, all couched in a similar vein, so apparently he was much the same in the red pepper days as he is today.

A year ago John B. Sheridan, a veteran St. Louis newspaperman, wrote this:

"Charles Comiskey is the greatest baseball man I have ever known."

Mr. Sheridan has had an opportunity to know them all, and as he has not always been eulogistic of the "Old Roman," his opinion may be regarded as impartial. He also knew him best in the days of the four-time winners.

And this from the pen of Charles W. Murphy, the man who ran a shoestring into a million, as owner of the Chicago Cubs:

"In my judgment he (Comiskey) is far and away the most famous figure ever connected with baseball since its start as a public amusement. But for him the rivalry between the National and American leagues, which has been a wonderful tonic for the sport, would never have been."

Murphy, who was a bitter rival of "Commy's" for years, could hardly be accused of writing the above to ingratiate himself, either with the "Old Roman" or with the newspaper for which he wrote it.

It has been the fixed purpose of the author from the first to permit the acts of "Commy" to pronounce their own eulogy and this shall be adhered to, yet the diversion above would serve as an alibi, if any are needed, for the superlatives, which have been used in commenting on his connection with the Browns. Comiskey has refrained in the past from writing a line of autobiography, and it is only by piecing together scraps of information from different sources that his real worth as a player and leader may be arrived at.

♦ CHAPTER VII ♦

The Revolt of the Brotherhood

Players and magnates lock horns and war follows—"Commy" parts company with Von der Ahe and puts team in Chicago—Big salary but no guarantee—Mike Kelly, a blank contract and $10,000—Brotherhood backers stampeded—Players' League goes to smash.

With the close of the 1889 season came the defection of the players and the virtual breaking up of the American Association and the National League. For Comiskey it meant the severing of partnership with Von der Ahe and his removal to his native city. The two became associated again for one year but the close relationship which had existed between them never was renewed even though Comiskey later overlooked the many slights the owner had put upon his manager from '87 on.

The causes leading up to the revolt were similar in character to those which had led to the formation of the American Association, viz., the dictatorial and arbitrary attitude of the National League, a course repeated ten years later, and which came near finishing the parent organization. Territorial restrictions, a stifling of competition and general greed, had precipitated war between the leagues. With the players, according to their own manifesto, only the latter figures.

Led by John M. Ward, now an attorney in New York, but in the early days a famous baseball player, there had been organized in 1885 "The National Brotherhood of Baseball Players," a fraternal organization, the declared purpose of which had to do with the individual players without reference to the owners. In the same year, however, the magnates passed a rule limiting player's salaries to $2,000 a year. When, after promises had been made, the owners failed to repeal the obnoxious limit, the dispute came to a head in the winter of 1889. The facts of the case were that the plan was elaborated on Spalding's trip around the world, something which came near being duplicated twenty-five years later on a similar world tour. The difference was that players figured in the first while envious magnates were the headliners in the second.

In a manifesto to the public the players explained their reasons for their revolutionary move. They made their principal attack on the reserve clause, while the alleged bad faith of the owners was not overlooked. The financial side and the integrity of the sport were made as prominent as possible with these words:

> There was a time when the League (National) stood for integrity and fair dealing. To-day it stands for dollars and cents. Once it looked to the elevation of the game and an honest exhibition of the sport; to-day its eyes are upon the turnstile. Men have come into the business for no other motive than to exploit it for every dollar in sight. Measures intended for the good of the game have been perverted into instruments for wrong.

This was answered in a lengthy counter-manifesto by the National League, the report being signed by A. G. Spalding, John B. Day and John I. Rogers, one of whom later proved the contention they made, that it was possible to go broke in the game. The telling argument in the answer was the revelation that in the five years just preceding, the eight club owners had drawn down only $150,000 in dividends while in that time the players had received $1,500,000 in salaries.

Regardless of words the issue was joined and the two organizations went into a clinch for the country's baseball patronage in the spring of 1890. It is enough to draw attention to the fact that the Chicago National League club lost ten of its most prominent players and New York twelve, to show how hard hit were the different teams. Anson, Burns and Hutchinson were the only ones left on the Chicago team, the "Cap" being deserted by Pfeffer, Dwyer, Tener, Bastian, Bartson, Darling, Farrell, Williamson, Ryan and Duffy.

The American Association was hit in equal proportion to the National and none suffered harder than Von der Ahe's club, which lost Comiskey, O'Neill, Latham, Boyle and King, the majority of whom went to make up the Chicago Brotherhood team of which Comiskey became captain and manager.

Ample backing was obtained for the Chicago team and a fine ball park was built at the corner of Wentworth avenue and 35th street. Twenty years later the captain-manager of the one-year team came into possession of the very grounds on which he and his fellow seceders cavorted in 1890. The imposing stand and other improvements of the early days had then disappeared, but it is likely that the cost of all would not have equaled the outlay for the fence which surrounds Comiskey Park of to-day.

The team which Comiskey was able to put into the field consisted of himself at first base, Fred Pfeffer at second, Charles Bastian and Ed Williamson at short, Arlie Latham at third, Jimmy Ryan, Hugh Duffy and Tip O'Neill in the outfield, Charles Farrell catcher and third base, Silver King, Mark Baldwin, Frank Dwyer and Charlie

Bartson, pitchers, and Jack Boyle, the star catcher. With this team "Commy" was unable to finish higher than fourth, which, better than anything else, demonstrated the class of the revolutionary cohorts. The Brotherhood teams wound up the season in the following order: Boston, Brooklyn, New York, Chicago, Philadelphia, Pittsburgh, Cleveland and Buffalo.

The question has frequently been asked why Comiskey quit the Browns when, to a man of his far-seeing vision, the venture must have been foredoomed to failure. His answer: "I couldn't do anything else and be on the level with the boys," admits of no argument. Comiskey had nothing to gain and everything to lose through the move. No one needed to write it down for him. He knew it before he separated himself from an assured $8,000 salary, which he was drawing from Von der Ahe, to accept an equal amount which, despite guarantees, might in the end turn into stage money.

The decision to cast his lot with the players came after he had been assured that he would be with a team in Chicago. It had been his ambition, ever since he first chase the ball on the prairies, to some day play on a regular team in his native city. He wanted to be among his former neighbors but fate decreed that another decade should intervene before he would be permanently "at home."

As is now history the Brotherhood program proved a fiasco all along the line, but to Comiskey the lesson was valuable. It became clear to him before the season ended that co-operative baseball was an impossibility and he kept this in mind and profited accordingly. He early discovered that player and promoter could not travel in the same harness. As the former had at best only a hazy idea of the financial end and the latter knew little or nothing of the technical side, clashes were bound to occur.

The players rightly argued that no one came through the turnstiles for a glimpse of the magnates. They themselves were the attrac-

tion, and this attitude lent itself to an impaired vision where the men on the field saw twice as many in the grandstand as the turnstiles tabulated. To them it was always a paying crowd, regardless of the "paper" represented, and thus the suspicion often got abroad that the capitalists "held out" on them. Having for many years traveled with baseball teams I can bear testimony to the fact

FRANK WING, cartoonist on the staff of the St. Paul *Dispatch*, and author of the well-known "The Fotygraft Album," is guilty of the above addition to the Comiskey gallery. Says Frank: "This here's Charley Comiskey, th' baseball man, when he lived here in St. Paul and managed th' Saints, as they call our team. Charley, he ust t' hang 'round Nick Weiler's place, down th' street here a ways, and play smear, ten cents a crack. He allus laid down a dollar, and ef he lost it, he quit, but ef he won, he kep' goin'. And one time, why Jim Donnelly, th' undertaker, he gits by th' police and drives his coffin wagon onto th' ball grounds when th' Saints was a-losin', and sings out: 'Hello, there, Charley! How's tricks?' Charley, he jist gives one look, then he calls a p'liceman over and says t' him: 'Git that there stiff-cart off'm these grounds before she hoodoos us fer keeps!' he says. The p'liceman, he gives pore old Jim th' run; and would yuh believe it? the Saints won th' game!"

that this visual defect still afflicts our present day heroes, and, it might be added, newspaper statisticians and fans as well.

So, in 1890, the leader of the Chicago Brotherhood team decided that in the future only one vote would be cast in any club that he was financially interested in. He adhered to this principle, even though the experiment in his minor league ventures proved costly and left him with a flattened pocketbook for his re-entry into Chicago.

It was not entirely the fault of the players that the Brotherhood failed. The immediate reason for the final breakup was the fact that some of the most enthusiastic backers wouldn't stay hitched. The New York and Brooklyn clubs, during the winter of '90–'91, entered into negotiations with the National League, a move which eventually had the effect of causing all the rest of the clubs to rush for cover.

The "selling out" process completed, it became theoretically a return to the ante-bellum status with the National League and the American Association still working under the agreement formulated in 1883. The players were to return to the clubs from which they originally hailed, and in 1891 Comiskey again became the head of the St. Louis Browns.

Hardly had the rival factions kissed and made up before war broke out anew. This time the National League and the American Association went into a clinch. The latter accused the former of bad faith in permitting the Pittsburgh and Boston clubs respectively to sign Bierbauer and Stovey. These players had originally been on the reserve list of the Philadelphia Athletics but, as it was claimed, had not appeared on the roster as turned out at the time of reorganization. After the Association had lost the case on appeal to the joint governing board, it announced the abrogation of the National Agreement and there started a fight to the finish.

To the credit of the game it should be pointed out that the players seldom lent themselves to the machinations of the magnates. Almost solidly they stood pat when it came to a question of honor, as was proven time and again during the reason. Few jumped from the Players' League to organized baseball but in each case wilful misrepresentation swayed them. How blandishment failed to influence others is related by A. G. Spalding himself, then at the head of the National League war committee.

According to Mr. Spalding it was figured that getting Mike Kelly back in the fold would be a ten strike and so he was approached. A $10,000 check and a blank contract were laid before him. The contract Spalding authorized Kelly to fill in himself. If he accepted he was to leave that night to join the Boston Nationals.

"His face blanched," writes Spalding in "America's National Game."

"Does that mean that I am to join the League?" Quit the Brotherhood? Go back on the boys?" queried Kelly.

"That's what it means," was the answer.

It must be remembered that Kelly always had had the reputation of being chronically broke, of continually depending on the club treasurer for an advance and it was a big temptation to "the King." He asked an hour and a half to think it over. Then he started for a walk but returned on time and made this announcement:

"I have decided not to accept. I want the $10,000 bad enough but I've thought the matter over and I can't go back on the boys."

Then he wound up the conversation, according to Mr. Spalding, by borrowing $500, but he never wavered in his allegiance to the Brotherhood.

With the new war under way the Association invaded Cincinnati for a starter and the franchise was turned over to A. L. Johnson, the Cleveland traction magnate. On the eve of the race Johnson sold the club to the National League, but the American Association succeeded in tying up in the court the $30,000 purchase money. The self-same Mike Kelly, who in the previous season had refused to sell out the Brotherhood, was put in charge of the team but failed to make good as a manager and the club proved a sporting and financial bloomer, the team being transferred to Milwaukee before the end of the season.

Nothing daunted by reverses Comiskey organized his motley crew in a last desperate effort to give St. Louis another pennant winner. By keeping a tight rein on the players and jollying the more and more eccentric Von der Ahe, he succeeded in holding the team together during that final season in St. Louis when raids by rival league clubs were of daily occurrence. Despite adversities which dogged his footsteps he landed the Browns in second place, Boston annexing the last championship of the old Association.

The Browns shuffled off with the following team: Jack Boyle and Tom Dolan, catchers; Clark Griffith and Jack Stivetts, pitchers; Charles Comiskey, first base; William Robinson, second base; Danny Lyons, third base; Shorty Fuller, short stop; W. E. Hoy, left field; Curt Welch, center field; Thomas McCarthy, right field.

The season left several of the American Association clubs on the financial rocks with as many of the National League in no better condition. The Association, though groggy, decided to carry on the fight the next year but the National, seeing a chance to get into undisputed possession of the field, conducted a series of secret "conversations" with the weakest of the flock. These prospered to the extent that in December of that year the deal for the amalgamation of the two leagues was consummated at Indianapolis.

The finishing touches included the buying out of four clubs for $135,000 and taking in the other four thus making a twelve-club circuit of the National League. A newly organized club in Chicago, headed by Fred Pfeffer, the former White Stocking and Brotherhood star and who is still making this city his home, was one of those absorbed. Those bought outright were Boston, Milwaukee, Columbus and Washington. Baltimore, St. Louis and Louisville became full fledged members of the older league as also did Washington, the latter franchise having been purchased by the Wagner Brothers, who had sold their Philadelphia club to the National League.

The double shift landed Comiskey with the National League for the first and only time, the maker of champions signing a three-year contract to manage the Cincinnati Reds for John T. Brush, who had gained control of the team in that marvelous shuffle at Indianapolis.

At this particular time Comiskey was bent on laying up something for a rainy day and Cincinnati represented the best pickings. He could no longer remain with Von der Ahe, who had acquired the fatal habit of regarding himself as a baseball man. Through diplomacy and the careful use of the influence he had acquired over him in the former days, Comiskey had succeeded in keeping "der boss president" at arms length during the final Association season but with the reorganization the two came to the parting of the ways.

The Association being no more, the National League presented the only opportunity, but it was with great reluctance that Comiskey marched under its banner. He was even free at that time with his opinion of the magnates, most of whom he cordially disliked. He did his best to give Cincinnati a winner but he never could become either enamored of, or accustomed to the peculiar brand of politics which regulated the affairs of the parent organization at that time.

Having grown up with it he always entertained a warm regard for the old Association and he could never forget the virtual scuttling of the craft, which partly accounted for the unbounded enthusiasm with which he entered the fray in 1900. To him the deed had had a touch of the piratical about it with the Jolly Roger replacing the emblem of sportsmen at the mast head. But with a family to support, sentimental considerations had to give way to the practical. Were he to move over to the camp of the enemy his tent would be pitched far away from the scenes of his former triumphs, and thus he transferred his chattels to Redland and St. Louis saw him no more.

♦ CHAPTER VIII ♦

"Commy" Becomes an Owner

Comiskey switches from brown to red stockings—Lands John T. Brush—Byron Bancroft Johnson is "discovered"—Western League is organized—"Commy" becomes his own boss—Spends five years in St. Paul as minor league magnate—"Izzy" and "Pat" in the lineup.

Cincinnati had been a member of the National league two years when Comiskey moved to the Queen City. It had gained little renown through the connection and the fans still referred with reverence to the surpassing days of 1869 and 1882, the former year having been made glorious by the unparalleled triumphs of the undefeated Red Stockings while the latter marked the period of the only pennant which had flown in Redland during two decades.

The success of the new manager was only mediocre. Although he did no better than his predecessors his record was no worse than those who followed him. Until the coming of Pat Moran, in this year of grace, 1919, Cincinnati has been the slough of despond for every manager except Charles Snyder, who led the team which captured the American Association pennant in 1882.

Many have speculated on the reason for the championless belt on the American baseball map, which embraces four cities—Washington, Cincinnati, Louisville and St. Louis. Connie Mack of the present-day Athletics and Clark Griffith of the Washington team collaborated to solve it and the solution was the weather, but neither could offer any explanation for the four time winners in St. Louis nor the fact that Louisville has been the cock of the walk in the new American Association.

"A team in St. Louis and Washington must be 25 percent better than any other in order to win a pennant," was Mack's deduction to which Griffith acquiesced.

"The heat in those cities has a weakening influence of the players and their strength is sapped before the middle of the season is reached," Mack is credited with having said.

Accepting this argument at its face value the old Browns must have been a wonderful aggregation. Taking it for granted that they were 25 percent stronger than any other team in the Association and tacking on the victories over Anson's wonderful legion and they must indeed have been a race of giants.

Neither Mack nor Griffith mentioned Cincinnati or Louisville but those who have had an opportunity to spend part of the heated season in either city, know well enough that they compare favorably with Washington and St. Louis. Comiskey himself does not attach undue importance to the hot weather theory and he does not believe that the weather had anything to do with his inability to win a flag for Cincinnati. That the mental atmosphere was not congenial may be taken for granted and that he worked for a man who knew little about the fine points of the game is matter of history.

John T. Brush, who succeeded to the ownership of the club in the winter of 1891, was best known as a successful clothing merchant although he had been the controlling factor in the Indianapolis Club of the National League and had fathered the classification salary rule which was the immediate cause of the players' revolt. Being an expert on woolens did not prevent Brush from rising to the eminence of the premier baseball politician in the National League and he was supreme in that field until his death.

The Brush tendency to pare down the salaries of the players, which had been inflated to a ruinous degree towards the close of the Eighties, was not parsimony but was a measure for the good of the league as a whole. Brush himself was as liberal in his dealings with his players as the majority of the magnates of his time, but his name was anathema to the rank and file, principally because of his lack of sympathy for the individual. He was pictured as imperious and wily and he was all of the latter but he lacked the attributes of a czar. Incidentally sporting writers dubbed him as the original "gumshoe" magnate in the game. Comiskey thought differently of his new boss and, although the majority of his personal friends were more or less at outs with the Cincinnati owner, who later became the controlling factor in the New York Giants, the "Old Roman" always insisted that the merchant-magnate was open and above-board in his dealings with everybody.

"Mr. Brush was one of the best men I ever worked for," said Comiskey, "and, although he could not be considered an expert so far as the playing end was concerned, he knew more about the game than the majority of the owners of his time, and what he did not know he was willing to learn from those who did. In the politics of the game he was in a class by himself, being one of the brainiest men ever connected with the sport.

"There was nothing stingy or mean about him, but there were few players who could put anything over on him. He always treated me with every consideration and when I left him he assured me that a place would be open for me as soon as I had gone broke. He tried his best to dissuade me from going to St. Paul, which he insisted was the graveyard among the minors, but having gotten used to cemeteries it was all the same to me. When he failed to change my mind he ended up our conversation with this remark:

"'When you are broke come back here and if, in the meantime, you need any help let me know.'

"The fact that he became the most uncompromising opponent of the American League later on does not detract from the estimation in which I hold his memory. Regardless of the enemies he made—our own league was solid against him, including myself—I still think of him as one of the biggest men that the game has produced."

The three-year "sentence" to Cincinnati was fraught with tremendous consequences for the sport. It was during this period that the plans for the American League—the organization which was to revolutionize baseball and make it truly national in character—were developed.

Prior to his coming to Ohio Comiskey had formed the acquaintance of a young newspaper man from Cincinnati, one Byron Bancroft Johnson, at that time sporting editor of Murat Halsted's Commercial Gazette. Johnson admired Comiskey both as a player and as a man, while the latter in turn recognized in the peppery writer qualities that were soon to make their imprint on the game. Johnson, however, was no worshipper of John T. Brush, regarding the Indianapolis merchant as an interloper and a factor inimical to the best interest of the sport. The dislike was mutual and, although later a formal truce was patched up, the feud between the two lasted until the death of Mr. Brush.

The sporting writer, younger in years than Cincinnati's newest guest, despite his distrust of the owner, never wavered in his allegiance to the manager. The partnership then formed has never been sundered and the mutual friendship was the basis for the prosperous condition of the sport today. The disagreements which have periodically come to the surface always have been more apparent than real and, regardless of personal differences which have developed, Johnson and Comiskey have stood shoulder to shoulder for the betterment of the game for almost a quarter of a century.

The antipathy, which Brush felt towards "Ban" eventually resulted in the formation of the rival league and Brush himself unconsciously became the biggest booster for the emerging Goliath. The trenchant pens which Johnson wielded gave the Indianapolis-Cincinnati magnate many an uneasy hour and he was not adverse to giving him other employment should the change take him out of Cincinnati. When Comiskey suggested to his employer that "Ban" would be a good man for the presidency of the Western League, Brush was torn by conflicting emotions. He would like to separate Johnson from his newspaper job if this could be accomplished without showing any favors. If the Western League position would keep him out of Cincinnati, well and good. If it should prove too big for him, so much the better, as in that case he would be discredited.

When the day arrived on which a choice would have to be made, Brush, who owned the Indianapolis club, missed his train. The other delegates considered Comiskey as representing the wishes of the Cincinnati magnate and cast their votes for Johnson and thus launched the career of one of the most remarkable executives that the baseball game has known.

Taking the moves which led up to the formation of the American League in their logical sequence, beginning with the organization of the Western League, the conviction is forced upon the historian that Comiskey was the real founder of the only rival that the old National League ever had.

As early as 1893 the "Old Roman" had mentally drafted an

enlarged Western League. It had its beginning on a trip in the South. After listening to tales of poverty poured into his ears by Southern League managers, Comiskey suggested to a number, all personal friends, that up North good baseball territory was going begging. They took him at his word and in the following year several moved their chattels across the Mason and Dixon line and the Western League came into being.

The circuit over which Johnson first presided in 1894 was modest in its scope and territory, consisting of Sioux City, Minneapolis, Milwaukee, Kansas City, Toledo, Indianapolis, Detroit and Columbus.

The real organizer being under contract to the Cincinnati club, was unable to realize his ambition of becoming an owner until his agreement with Brush expired. Immediately after the 1894 season he bought the Sioux City franchise and moved the team, or what was left of it, to St. Paul. The good wishes of Brush went with his manager, although he did his best to persuade "Commy" not to make the leap. An even more attractive contract than he had enjoyed was put before him, but the manager turned down a sure thing for the dubious privilege of becoming his own boss.

The St. Paul venture made "Commy" rich in experience but poor in purse. The size of his bank roll necessitated rigid economy and the strength of the team was in direct ratio to the resources back of it. He did not make a splurge, but endeavored to break even.

It has always been the contention of Comiskey that the only useful owner in baseball has been the one who has been through the mill as a player and manager, and the sentiment has not been in disparagement of that host of sportsmen-capitalists who have had a hand in upbuilding the game. It is simply a conviction with "Commy," born from experience.

"There has been many a good loser in baseball who never slid into a base," commented Comiskey once, "but the man I would rather

One of the greatest combinations of stars ever put together—Comiskey's Chicago Brotherhood team of 1890.

see behind a club when it means a fight to a finish is one who learned the game on the field. That kind of man will stand to lose his last dollar without a whimper while one who regards the game as an investment is generally among the first to pull out. Sentiment must have equal weight with business judgment."

A choice story supporting this theory was circulated in the early days of the American League, when Ban Johnson would turn up with a new bunch of capitalist-backers at every meeting.

VIII. "Commy" Becomes an Owner

There had been a change of owners in Detroit and the enthusiastic "Ban" was congratulating the rest of the magnates over the acquisition of Samuel F. Angus, who was a power in the financial world. Comiskey listened intently and then, probably having in mind his experiences in the Brotherhood days when some of the wealthiest backers of the players were first to run for cover, dryly remarked:

"One more millionaire will break the American League."

"Commy" never has changed his viewpoint and that is why he has always been willing to back practical baseball men to the limit of his ability, while avoiding entangling alliances with men of money. It is doubtful if there is any other owner in baseball who has backed more minor league clubs than has Comiskey. It has been a habit with him when some of his veteran players have started to slip to offer them their choice of some minor league club. I know that this happened on at least three different occasions.

"Go out and pick your club and I will back you," would be "Commy's" injunction. "If you make any money it is yours; if there is a deficit at the end of the season I will make it up."

As the player-manager was assured a regular salary there could be no risk.

Comiskey himself enjoyed no such assurances when he went to St. Paul in 1895. With him it was sink or swim. Everything he had was invested in the club, and the equipment of his ball park compelled him to become chummy with the bankers. He organized the best team that his resources permitted, with himself as captain, manager and president. When necessary he also played first base.

His best years in St. Paul were his first and his last—1895 and 1899. In each of these seasons he finished second after flag races which still are talked about in the Northwest. The club did poorly in 1896, but moved up to third position in 1897. The following year found the Saints in fourth place.

"Commy's" first season in St. Paul was one to try his soul. After his first trip, on which he lost seventeen straight games, he returned home to find that an injunction had been issued against him preventing Sunday games on the grounds on which he was then playing. A reporter on a local paper broke the news to him on his return to the city.

"Oh, is that all," commented Comiskey. "They have only stopped me from playing one day a week. I didn't know but that they would restrain me from playing on the other six."

Then after building a new "Sunday park" he whipped his team into winning condition and finished second at the end of the season.

While in St. Paul Comiskey picked up two recruits who later figured prominently in major league pennant races. These were Frank Isbell and Roy Patterson. "Izzy" in time justified "Commy's" judgment by becoming one of the great first basemen of the game, while Patterson did more than his share in winning the first two flags for the "Old Roman," by his pitching.

Taking few into his confidence Comiskey applied his mind to expansion as soon as he assumed the title of president. Needing more time to plan, and finding that his executive duties interfered with his playing, first base saw him less and less. He put on his uniform for the last time in 1898, after eighteen years on the initial corner, winding up his career as the most finished first sacker of his time.

◆ CHAPTER IX ◆

White Sox and War

American League is born—Spalding furnishes brief for new rival—Comiskey enters Chicago and encounters opposition from the National League—Baseball historians explain reasons for invasion—Telegram by Johnson immediate cause of break—Battles in court follow.

An unyielding attitude on the part of the National League hastened the entry of rival teams into Chicago and other major league cities. It compelled Comiskey later to declare for open warfare against some of his best friends. He preferred to expand along more peaceful lines. The financial risks were great. The ruins of the old Association, the Union and Brotherhood leagues still blurred the baseball horizon. Yet out of the wreckage of blasted hopes and dissipated fortunes there still remained something to be salvaged—sentiment.

Without attributing too great a measure of altruistic motives to the founders of the American League, it was this asset which was capitalized to the full by its organizers. Appeals to the fans to help save the game were combined with business sagacity, a certain amount of bluff and elastic bank accounts. Also into the new league came men who were in the prime of life, quick on the mental trigger and whirlwinds in action. These were more than a match for the older heads and proved adept in taking advantage of every false move of the older organization.

No one has presented a more effective brief for the American League nor vindicated its promoters better than one who was allied with the opposition—A. G. Spalding, famed as a player, manager, owner and merchant. In explaining "Freedmanism," which at this particular time was rampant in the National League, he penned these words in his book "America's National Game":

> Some years before the opening of the Twentieth Century the National League had begun to lose prestige with the public. This loss of caste was not due to a failure on the part of the league to correct abuses. It had achieved wonders in that respect. It had absolutely driven out gambling and gamblers.... It had done away with the drinking evil....
>
> The trouble now was not with gamblers or with players, but with club officials, generally termed "magnates," and it will be readily understood how difficult a matter it was to deal with them. Especially was it hard to reach cases where there was no actual violation of baseball law—just personal cussedness and disregard for the future welfare of the game.
>
> Soon after the American sport became established as a national pastime, and was showing for its promoters a balance on the right side of the ledger, a certain clique came into the league for purposes of pelf. They at once let it be known by their acts that they were in baseball for what they could get out of it. They were absolutely devoid of sentiment, cared nothing for the integrity or perpetuity of the game beyond the limits of their individual control thereof. With these men it was simply a mercenary question of dollars and cents. Everything must yield to the one consideration of inordinate greed.

Comiskey never missed an opportunity of "kidding" the opposition magnates on their slippery tactics when the opportunity offered. After the first joint meeting between the two leagues August Herrmann of Cincinnati, who had only lately come into the organization, exclaimed, with some show of perturbation while standing in the lobby of a New York hotel, that he had lost his watch.

"Well, Garry, don't get excited about it," said Comiskey. "You will get used to it. Didn't you just come out of a National League session?"

In addition to internal feuds and distrust among the members, the National League had been burdened with a twelve-club incubus. With the expiration of the ten-year agreement in 1900 plans had been set on foot to reduce the circuit to eight clubs. This move had been anticipated by Comiskey, Johnson and their partners and they planned to take advantage of the readjustment. In the reorganization Cleveland, Baltimore, Louisville and Washington were abandoned by the National. The Western offered to buy the National property in Cleveland if it would be permitted to put a club in Chicago. There was ready acquiescence in the former proposal but violent opposition developed to the placing a club in Chicago by Comiskey. It was at this juncture that Ban Johnson started his campaign of "education" and Comiskey his of good fellowship.

Frequent meetings in Chicago, which was made the real headquarters of the new American League, as it had been of the old Western, offered opportunities of getting the case before the public. Except that each city was promised a winner, the financial end was subordinated to the sentimental and, to the everlasting credit of the American League founders and those who followed, this has been kept to the fore from that day to this. Many may differ but the present high standard of the sport justifies the conclusions reached.

At the first rumblings of invasion magnates in the National prepared for the fray. They were in no condition to fight, due mainly to costly rows among themselves, and thus it early simmered down to a game of bluff. At this two could play and among the champion performers could be counted the former Cincinnati sporting writer.

At the time Comiskey first publicly broached his intention of putting a club in Chicago James A. Hart was president of the National League club there. Hart and Comiskey were well acquainted. The former had been secretary of the old Louisville Association team while Comiskey was manager of the Browns. He was one of the wheelhorses of the National and knew the politics of the game from A to Z. He was also one of the few who sensed the plans of the new league but, as he afterwards admitted, he failed to gauge their actual effect on baseball in general.

Knowing Comiskey as he did Hart was positive in his own mind, as he expressed it to the writer, that once the American landed in Chicago it would only be a matter of time before the old league would find rival teams in the majority of its cities. This fear was an incentive to him in trying to keep Comiskey out of Chicago, his argument against admission being based on what was regarded as an axiom in the National that no city could support two ball clubs.

Mr. Hart lived to see two clubs prosper in Chicago, with the receipts of each far in excess of those which obtained when a single club was the rule. Mr. Hart retired from the game before the experiment had actually been put to a lasting test. He died while this volume of reminiscences of his greatest rival was being written. He passed away with no animosity towards the "Old Roman," whom he freely conceded was one of the commanding figures in baseball.

Frequent conferences during the winter of 1900 between Comiskey and Hart failed to effect a working agreement, although the former had, from the beginning, announced that he would put a club in Chicago. Naturally the majority of Hart's fellow owners made his case their own and the threat was conveyed to the American League that protection would be withdrawn were the organization to persist in invading reserved territory. President Johnson's intimation that his clubs were in no need of guardianship and that they stood ready to withdraw from the National Agreement had its effect. The National "caved" and Comiskey was legally admitted.

The fact that Comiskey had already leased a field and practically closed the contract for his stand showed how much he was influenced by the pending negotiations. At the last moment President Hart succeeded in getting in an "amendment" to the effect that the American League team should not use the name "Chicago." To Comiskey this was of small consequence as he well knew that, if worthy of the honor, the fans would soon do their own christening. Besides, he had long before decided that his team should be known as "White Stockings," an appellation which was later contracted into "White Sox," a form better suited to the exigencies of newspaper headline writing.

Baseball historians have often been hard put to find a real motive for the expansion of the Western into the American League, In "The National Game," A. H. Spink suggests that in reality the American League was the outgrowth of an organization which he and his fellow enthusiasts tried to form in 1898 and 1899 for the purpose of putting new life and energy into the sport which was sadly on the decline.

Francis C. Richter in his "History and Records of Baseball," contends that the leading figures in the Western League, foreseeing the breakup of the National League twelve-club circuit, simply took advantage of existing conditions.

George L. Moreland in his "Balldom," lays the formation of the second major league to the keenness of the Western owners to get into more populous cities although their vision did not go beyond Chicago, Cleveland and Detroit. The later expansion, says Mr. Moreland, was dictated by the desire of the new organization to help out the National by heading off a threatened American Association.

A. G. Spalding indirectly gives his explanation in his essay on "Freedmanism," but is otherwise silent on the subject.

The opinions entertained, although differing somewhat, are not necessarily contradictory, as each partially explains the reason for the organization of the American League. The real reason is not to be found in the paragraphs just quoted.

I was present in my newspaper capacity at the meetings held in Chicago during 1898 and 1899. It is true that leading figures in the Western League were present but purely as spectators. There was at no time any intention on the part of Comiskey, Johnson, Loftus and others to ally themselves with those who deliberated over the formation of a rival to the National League, as their own plans had already been formulated. They were only waiting for the opportune moment, which they knew would come with the revision of the National League circuit.

Back of it all was a deeper motive for the formation of the American League. When Comiskey, through force of circumstances, was forced out of Chicago after the collapse of the Players' League in 1890, he made the mental determination that one day the old organization would have competition in Chicago. Consequently the inference that the American League invasion was dictated by temporary expedients is erroneous. The move had been conceived by Comiskey nine years before its actual consummation. The fact that the National greased the way has nothing to do with the case.

It is a part of the secret history of baseball that Comiskey had a chance to locate in Chicago in 1891. With the breakup of the Brotherhood, A. G. Spalding suggested to the then manager of the Players' League team that he continue to play on the grounds where the players went broke in 1890. Spalding seemed to have had only a hazy idea as to what organization Comiskey should tie up to, although the American Association was suggested. With the suggestion went the proposal that A. C. Anson should take complete charge of the team on the West Side.

"I told Mr. Spalding that as I was making my living in baseball it made no difference to me where I played," said Comiskey in relating the incident. "When, however, he suggested that I had to rely on my own finances I concluded that I would rather work for someone else."

It is not necessary to look for justification for a second club in Chicago. If any is needed sentiment and business judgment provide the answer. Chicago was Comiskey's home. To locate there meant everything to the minor league magnate. Chicago was the pivot of the American League venture. Invasion of other cities would be a logical sequence and expansion was, in the minds of the original promoters, never dependent on the whims of those who controlled the National. The program was for a second major league—without a conflict, if possible; war to the hilt if necessary, but a national organization at all hazards.

Plans having been perfected the organization and expansion were mere matters of detail—such as for instance the raising of a few hundred thousand dollars. As Comiskey had "discovered" Johnson, so the latter dug up Charles W. Somers. Somers was a baseball fan in Cleveland—one of those enthusiasts who went to bed with a baseball guide under his pillow. In addition to having his head crammed full of averages Mr. Somers had a bank account which, at this juncture, was of great importance.

While Somers' partner in the Cleveland club, John F. Kilfoyle, looked after the home team during the season of 1900, Somers, Johnson and Comiskey mapped out a course of action. The bankroll was transferred to Boston and Somers became owner of the new

American League club there in 1901. His credit aided one or two others but as soon as local capital could be obtained he pulled out of every city except his own.

Somers remained as one of the commanding figures of the game until financial reverses, not connected with baseball, overtook him. He held the office of vice president of the American League up to a few years ago when the owner of the White Sox was elected to the position.

Of those who were present at the birth of the American League in 1900 only two still are connected with it—President Johnson and Charles A. Comiskey. Those who went in to buck the National as presidents of their respective clubs in 1900 were: Chicago, Comiskey; Cleveland, John F. Kilfoyle; Detroit, James D. Burns; Indianapolis, W. H. Watkins; Milwaukee, Matt Killilea; Buffalo, James Franklin; Minneapolis, Clarence Saulpaugh; Kansas City, James H. Manning.

In order to confer the distinction of an honorable "ancestry" on the American League historians have endeavored to link the junior major organization with certain predecessors of more or less renown. Age might give it a greater respectability but the fact remains that it was the Western League, founded in 1894 which was expanded into the American League in 1900. The original Northwestern League, organized in 1879, and the Western Association, founded in 1888, cannot claim relationship.

As was to be expected the American League did not take the country by storm during the first season—principally because it was still pretty much confined to the West. The well matured plan to invade the East became public soon after the close of the first year. The matter was brought to a head by the American League purposely neglecting to renew its application for protection under the National Agreement. In answer to a telegram of inquiry from President Young of the National League, President Johnson of the American, sent

Comiskey's first American League team in Chicago: pennant-winners in 1900. Upper row, left to right: Fisher, Dillard, Isbell, Denzer, Patterson. Middle row: Brain, Hartman, Padden, Comiskey, Shearon, Sugden, Wood. Lower row: O'Leary, Shugart, Hoy, H. McFarland.

this answer which precipitated the greatest war in the history of the game:

> The plan of the American League to occupy eastern territory has been well defined and I think the men of the National League thoroughly understand our position in the matter.
>
> For two years we have been menaced by the possible formation of a league hostile to our interest and detrimental in many ways to organized baseball. This annual agitation is hurtful and

> we proposed to so shape our organization as to check it in the future.
>
> In extending our circuit to the far east, it is unreasonable to assume we could continue along the old lines prescribed by the National Agreement. New conditions must alter, in part, our relations with the National League. This is a matter I have discussed informally with some of our members.

In this message from Johnson is found the basis for the claim that the American League expanded because it was threatened by a rival organization. This is refuted when it is called to mind that in reality the "new" American Association was fostered by the National in the hope that it would serve to head off the ambitious rival.

With the gauntlet thrown down Indianapolis, Kansas City and Minneapolis were replaced by Philadelphia, Baltimore and Washington. There was no threat made to put a club into either Boston or New York, as the circuit committee, consisting of Comiskey, Johnson and Somers, believed that the parent organization would accept the inevitable and make overtures for reconciliation. This hope not being realized and the National having made it known that it was on a "war footing" Buffalo was eliminated and Boston added.

The issue being joined the two organizations went into a death grapple with no quarter given or asked on either side. The first move of the American League, after locating in the East, was to organize a raid on the playing talent of the older league. This was blocked for a time by the Players' Protective Association which held to the rule of "Prior Contracts." The ban was soon lifted and the shifting began.

The National sought recourse in the courts, a procedure which resulted in diametrically opposite opinions from the bench. The only legal hurdle of consequence was raised in Pennsylvania where Lajoie, Bernhardt and Fraser, who had signed with Connie Mack's Athletics, were enjoined from playing with any other team than the

Philadelphia National League club. The players being unable to come to terms all three signed with the Cleveland Club. Lajoie was paid the highest salary ever received by a ball player up to that time—$24,000 for three years. After the first raid the following players made up the different American League clubs with the exception of Chicago:

ATHLETICS—Bernhardt, Platt, Plank, Fraser, Wiltse, Ketchem, pitchers; Powers, Leahey, Steelman, Milligan, Smith, catchers; Lajoie, Davis, Cross, Dolan, Ely, Geier, Murphy, infielders; Seybold, Fultz, McIntyre, Heyden, outfielders. Manager, Connie Mack.

WASHINGTON—Patton, Gear, Mercer, Carrick, Lee, Jordan, pitchers; Clarke, Grady, catchers; Dungan, Everett, Quinn, Coughlin, Clingman, infielders; Waldron, Farrell, O'Brien, Foster, Luskey, outfielders.

CLEVELAND—Wood, Moore, Scott, Hoffer, Hart, Bracken, Cristall, Dowling, McNeal, pitchers; Yeager, Woods, Connor, McGuire, catchers; LaChance, Beck, Bradley, McQuade, Sheibeck, Shay, infielders; Genins, Harvey, McCarthy, Pickering, Donovan, O'Brien, outfielders.

BOSTON—Lewis, Cuppy, Winters, Mitchell, Young, Kellum, Foreman, pitchers; Criger, Schreckongost, Beville, McLean, catchers; Freeman, Ferris, J. Collins, Parent, infielders; Stahl, Dowd, Hemphill, Jones, outfielders.

DETROIT—Miller, Yeager, Cronin, Seiver, Owens, Frisk, pitchers; Shaw, Buelow, McAllister, catchers; Dillon, Gleason, Casey, Elberfeld, Crackett, infielders; Barrett, Nance, Holmes, outfielders.

BALTIMORE—McGinnity, Nops, Foreman, Howell, Kearne, Dunn, Yerkes, Schmidt, pitchers; Robinson, Bresnahan, catchers; Donlin, Hart, Foutz, Williams, McGraw, Keister, infielders; Jackson, Brodie, Seymour, Rohe, outfielders.

MILWAUKEE—Dowling, Garvin, Reidy, Sparks, Husting, Hawley, pitchers; Maloney, Donohue, Connor, Leahey, catchers; Anderson, Friel, Conroy, Gilbert, Burke, infielders; Duffy, Geier, Hallman, Jones, Hogriever, Bruyette, Waldron, outfielders.

♦ CHAPTER X ♦

Players' Bench to Swivel Chair

Comiskey locates club on South Side in Chicago—Wins a pennant and says farewell to the bench—Open war between leagues break out—Still another flag for the White Sox—Fielder Jones takes command—"Iron Man" Walsh gets into the picture.

It would be an exaggeration to contend that Comiskey entered Chicago in the spring of 1900 with a great team. It would not be in accordance with the facts to maintain that he moved into a palatial ball park. The majority of his players had cavorted on the St. Paul minor league diamond. His plant was put up under pressure of double shifts and in construction and looks suffered accordingly.

As pointed out Comiskey had leased the grounds and drawn the plans for the grand stand and bleachers before he had been legally admitted. The real estate was located at Thirty-ninth street and Princeton avenue, the lot of land having been the home of the Chicago Cricket Club for years. There were no stands or buildings worthy of the name but the smooth turf made an ideal playing field.

A late winter greatly interfered with the building of the grand stand but, the new magnate being a son of "Honest John" Comiskey, union artisans waived many of the rules and by working in daylight, dark and on Sundays, the seats were in place for the initial game April 21. The united efforts produced a plant which, although far from being an architectural symphony, had the utilitarian advantage of capacity and fresh air. The grand stand was raised high off the ground, affording a view from beneath, while a ticklishly balanced roof served as a haven for the reporters.

For transportation the fans depended mainly on the Wentworth avenue surface line, the cross town line on Thirty-ninth and the South Side Elevated railroad, four blocks away.

It had been predicted that the South Side would prove a morgue for any league team, as South Siders had never given any evidence of taking kindly to the national pastime. The Brotherhood team had failed to draw and when the Chicago Nationals had played part of their games in the park of the former, which it had taken over, President Hart had found the experiment costly. The teeming west Side had been the baseball center of Chicago from the inception of the game, a fact of which Comiskey was well aware.

Despite gloomy prediction a new chapter was written with the very first tilt. A capacity crowd greeted the invaders. The Sox did not fill the park every day but at the end of the season Comiskey was in condition to buy up some of the outstanding stock, which he had been compelled to distribute. So well did the fans rise to the occasion that only a few years elapsed before he had become the sole owner of the club and a few more seasons sufficed to finance a new baseball plant, second to none in the country.

With Comiskey on the bench as manager, the White Sox pulled through and, in a tight race, won the first pennant of the American League, the figures reading 82 won and 53 lost for a percentage of .607. Milwaukee was second, four games behind and in order came Indianapolis, Detroit, Kansas City, Cleveland, Buffalo and Minneapolis.

The team which captured the flag was composed of Denzer, Fisher, Katoll, and Patterson, pitchers; Buckley, Sugden and Wood, catchers; Isbell, first base; Padden, field captain and second base; Hartman, third base; Shugart, short stop; Hoy, Dillard, H. McFarland, Brodie and Shearon, outfielders.

It could not by any stretch of imagination be called a fast outfit. In fact it was probably the slowest aggregation that ever worked under the "Old Roman," but it was fairly effective with the bat. Strategy was furnished from the bench. Of the pitchers, Denzer and Patterson did the best work while Sugden was an experienced catcher. Padden, a star second baseman, was slowing up as were several of the others. Although of a minor league calibre it was as game a bunch as ever stepped on the ball field and the rapidly increasing throng in the stands found it more and more to their interest to stick until the end of the ninth inning.

A major league aggregation took the field the following year. War having broken out, the winter was spent in raiding the enemy's preserves. These are the more aristocratic names found in the 1901 lineup:

Pitchers, Clark Griffith, Jimmy Callahan, Wiley Piatt, Roy Patterson, John Katoll; catchers, Billy Sullivan and Joe Sugden; infielders, Frank Isbell, Sam Mertes, Frank Hartman, Ed Burke, Frank Shugart; outfielders, William Hoy, Fielder Jones, Clarence Foster, Ed McFarland.

With the signing of Griffith, Callahan and Mertes, civil war was on. All three were stars of the first magnitude and their migration from the West Side of Chicago to the South Side accentuated the cleavage between the two camps. National League fans took it much to heart. A bitter rivalry sprang up, which continued until followers of each discovered that even with two teams there could be enough glory to go around.

X. Players' Bench to Swivel Chair

With the close of the 1900 season Comiskey said farewell to the bench, planted himself in the presidential chair and turned the managerial reins over to Clark Griffith. The veteran quit with a record of seventeen years behind him as manager. In that time he had won five pennants and one world's championship. He closed a professional career that had extended over 25 years, having been in uniform all but two. When he stepped from the dug-out he was in his prime—42 years of age—and his physical condition was such that he threatened to break into the game now and then.

"If he does he will show the rest of us up," was Isbell's sage comment.

It was a pretty good team which took the field in 1901, the first year of the war, but it had to be. There was plenty of competition all the way from Boston to Milwaukee. The list of players given in the preceding chapter gives a fair idea of the "class," but after another stirring race Chicago again won, with Boston second, four games behind. Detroit, Athletics, Baltimore, Washington, Cleveland and Milwaukee finished in order named.

On paper, at least, two clubs seemed to have the edge on the White Sox—Boston and the Athletics. Chicago had increased its speed by the acquisition of Callahan, Jones, Mertes and Hoy, but it was far from being a fast combination. In hitting it was only superior to the team of the year before but it pulled through on its pitching and team work, the battle raging to the end of the season.

With the ring cleared for the free-for-all in 1902 the new league found it convenient to replace Milwaukee with St. Louis in the circuit. As the Mound City had boasted two clubs within its gates at different times the transfer did not create a sensation, but the defection of Baltimore, in the middle of the season, did. The onus for the smash was placed on John McGraw, who was the leader of the Orioles at the time. He resigned in July to become manager of the New

York Nationals and, a month later, the majority stockholders sold the team to John T.Brush, who that spring had obtained control of the Giants. Of the team McGinnity, Cronin, McGann and Bresnahan followed McGraw, while Kelley and Seymour were released to Cincinnati.

Brush had been the man to engineer the deal and he had figured that the strategy would have the effect of breaking up Johnson's circuit or at least would force the invaders to come to terms. He never made a greater mistake. Some of the weak-kneed members in the American League were for a compromise.

"Let it be a fight to a finish," demanded Comiskey in Chicago.

The league as a whole went to the rescue of the plucked Orioles and a makeshift team was put in the field and finished the season. At the close President Johnson took advantage of the alleged underground methods employed by the National to inflame the fans against the parent body and thus secured a following in the country's metropolis which later was taken advantage of to the full. When the New York invasion finally took place the American League circuit committee, still in good working order, fortified itself by drafting backers for the new club from the leading political, social and financial lights of the city.

The elimination of Baltimore and the entry into New York provided the American League's missing link, completed an organization which has not seen a territorial change up to the present, and eventually led to peace and a new National Agreement.

The invectives hurled at Brush during this period by supporters of the junior organization were as emphatic as they were picturesque. Comiskey did not join in the chorus. The turn of affairs made baseball enemies of the "Old Roman" and the New York magnate, but the Chicago owner always insisted that Brush was not as bad as painted.

"It is his method of warfare," Commy would explain to the interviewer. "We have ours and we will whip them at the gate. There is the place to decide the fight."

Comiskey was right. The clicking of the turnstiles and the daring incursions into the players' fold decided the fray. At the end of the 1902 season came overtures for peace. With Harry C. Pulliam as president of the National League it was not difficult to reach an agreement, which was signed at Cincinnati, January 10, 1903.

With the new compact baseball was put on a solid foundation and the structure was not again to be disturbed until a decade had passed.

It is not the intention to go into the details of each pennant race which followed the first year of actual warfare. Only the high spots in the career of the White Sox will be touched upon. The statistics of the game may be safely left to the many excellent baseball "guides."

New names are to be found on the 1902 White Sox roster in Garvin, McMackin, Eddie Hughes, Leitner, Durham, Eddie McFarland, Daly, Strang and Green—the latter "Danny" of the Cubs. Several others were tried out but found wanting. The name of George Davis also appears for the first time. Davis had twice been manager of the Giants and, although well along in playing years, was considered one of the best infielders in the game. The veteran braced up the infield but other teams also had been greatly strengthened through new raids and the best the Sox could do was to finish fourth to the Athletics. St. Louis and Boston were second and third respectively, while Cleveland, Washington, Detroit and Baltimore trailed Chicago.

The newcomers on the 1903 White Sox team, after the final foray into the enemy's territory, were Flaherty, White, Dunkle, Owen and Altrock, pitchers; Slattery, catcher; Dolan, Tannehill,

Magoon and Clarke, infielders, and Hallman, outfielder. To Griffith was assigned the task of piloting the new Gotham team and Jimmy Callahan succeeded his former teammate as manager. Through a combination of circumstances, with injuries predominating, the Sox became the American League doormat, being unable to finish better than seventh, Boston capturing the flag. The Athletics, Cleveland, New York, Detroit and St. Louis were above Chicago, while Washington alone trailed it.

This year saw the first of the Sox-Cubs series for the city championship. It proved the longest, in point of games, bar one, which either had engaged in, fourteen games being crowded into the first two weeks of October. Each won seven, the series terminating in a draw. Comiskey was insistent on playing the fifteenth, but Frank Seele, manager of the Cubs, demurred. He gave as the reasons that the contracts with the players had expired and that Joe Tinker, his star short stop, had a date at the altar in Kansas City.

The historic gameness of the Sox again came to the front in this series. The Cubs were getting a long lead in games early. Altrock turned the scales. He was not, at this time, considered much of a pitcher, and had been given only a minor part. When all the star Sox pitchers had been walloped Nick volunteered.

"Give me a chance," he pleaded with Callahan. "I can lick them. I have as much as I always had—my glove—and that's enough."

Altrock pitched and won.

The year 1904 was marked by the appearance with the White Sox of Edward Walsh, a giant in size but of small attainments as a ball player. He had been drafted from the Newark club of the Eastern League, where he rejoiced in the sobriquet of "Iron Man." He was all of that when he first reported to the spring training camp at Marlin, Texas, but that exhausted his repertoire. He had speed to burn but didn't know how to use it. He was impossible as a fielder and a bunt hit in his direction was always good for at least one base.

Coal mining around Plains, Pennsylvania, in his early days had failed to stunt his physique, and "Apollo" proved no misnomer. When, however, he came to carry out the role of the Grecian divinity aside from music and oratory, Walsh fell afoul of the "Old Roman." Posing had never been an attribute of "Commy." It was an art with Walsh. On the point of delivering the ball he sometimes would stand for a minute or more, with arms poised on high, shoulders thrown back, one foot a step in front of the other and all the time never moving a muscle. Coming off the field one day Comiskey accosted him.

"That's a great pose you got, Ed," began the Sox boss, "but I don't think you keep it long enough. When you get your arms above your head hold the position until they get the cameras ready."

Walsh saw the point, but never entirely dropped the pose. Later on he used it to develop a throw to bases, especially first, that had every runner in the league "buffaloed." The victims of the deadly snap throw insisted that it was "balk" motion, but Ed got away with it, as no umpire had the heart to interfere with a maneuver which was the acme of artistic deception.

Having looked him over once both Callahan and Comiskey came to the conclusion that Walsh had been a whale among minnows and that he should be given the opportunity of resuming the role. Yet, somehow or other, he was retained. An incident, considered of no moment at the time, turned the scales in his favor and eventually made him one of the greatest hurlers of all time.

In the Sox camp at Marlin was a pitcher by name of Elmer Stricklett. He was the opposite to Walsh in build, and yet he handed up a ball to the batters in practice which was unhittable. It took twists and turns in approaching the plate that were against all the

A "family group" of the Sox-Giants world tourists in front of the Sphinx. Mr. and Mrs. Comiskey may be seen in the center, mounted on "ships of the desert."

laws of gravity. Everybody took a swing at it. Most of them missed it, sometimes by a foot or more. Billy Sullivan, catching, found the ball wet and slippery.

"What's the idea," demanded the backstop, who was not enamored of handling the sphere.

"Oh, that's my way of pitching," explained Stricklett.

"What do you call it?" insisted Sullivan.

"Don't know," was the answer. "I suppose 'spitball' explains it as well as anything."

No one watched the gyrations of the ball closer than did Ed

Walsh. Curiously enough Stricklett hailed from the same club as did Walsh, although Elmer had preceded the "Iron Man" a couple of years. It was while he was with the Newark club that Stricklett had been taught the delivery by Pitcher Corridon of the Philadelphia Nationals. Corridon only possessed the rudiments of the delivery. He knew it combined a drop and curve, both in and out, yet he never could control it. Stricklett started to perfect it while with the Brooklyn club. When he joined the White Sox he had mastered it fairly well, but before he could show its effectiveness he developed a lame arm and was released. He is credited with having pitched one game for the White Sox. His pupil figured in 415 games and it was not until 1913 that he complained of a sore wing.

Walsh continued to grow as a pitcher, but slowly at first. It was not until 1906 that he got into his real stride. In that year he pitched in 41 games. In 1908 he figured in 66, a record for the league. Then in successive years he rolled up a record of 32, 45, 55 and 62. He became the master of the moist delivery and the idol of the fans. Even Comiskey became reconciled to his "pose." Bonuses, autos and other tokens of value were showered on him.

Heroes make friends. Walsh's were legion. He could have dispensed with many to his own advantage. While at the height of his career some of his self-appointed advisors suggested that he didn't get enough money from Comiskey.

"Stand out for $7,500," was the advice.

It was suggested that he put his affairs in the hands of a lawyer. The attorney wrote one letter to Comiskey. He never repeated as "Commy" answered the first as only he could do.

"So Walsh has a lawyer now," said Comiskey at the receipt of the epistle. "He didn't need one during the three years I was paying him to sit on the bench and learn something about pitching."

Walsh got a job coaching a college team after he heard from

his friend the attorney. When he didn't hear anything from Comiskey he jumped on a train, came to Chicago and signed the contract laid in front of him. It was for less money that he would have received had he been without "legal advice."

That fall he was handed a check for $3,000 to be applied towards the education of his two boys. Reports to the contrary, Walsh was paid one of the highest salaries of any player in the league. It did not always figure in the contract, but he got it just the same.

Came the time, in the spring of 1913, when Walsh switched from a baseball to a medicine ball. It was at Paso Robles, California. He tossed the big leather sphere once too often. Something snapped in his shoulder and he was through as a pitcher. For three years he sat on the bench practically useless to the team. Comiskey spent a small fortune in trying to rehabilitate him. Bone setters and masseurs lived in clover while the experiment was going on, but the mighty hurler never again pitched a game in his old-time form.

Through as a pitcher Comiskey offered him a minor league club. Walsh hated to think that he couldn't "come back," and turned it down. His last trial was with the American Association. He failed. Coming into Comiskey's office that summer he admitted that his career as a ball player was over.

"I knew you were through years ago," said Comiskey, "but you are still on the White Sox pay roll. I need a good scout."

Contemporaneous with Walsh was Frank Smith, another giant. He had all the earmarks of a great pitcher. Also some peculiarities. One of these was a windup with men on the bases, which carried all the frills of an acrobatic feat. Callahan tried to change his style, but to no purpose. Comiskey, finally becoming exasperated, called Smith in.

"When a man on first is trying to steal, while you are pitching, the catcher must throw the ball to third base instead of second," said Comiskey with mock seriousness.

"But why?" innocently asked the big twirler.

"Because when you get through your windup the runner ought to be sliding into that bag," answered the "Old Roman."

Donohue also appeared for the first time on this trip to Marlin—the immortal Jiggs, who after a disappointing start became the most finished first baseman of the decade. Then there were Berry and Heydon, catchers; Dundon and Rossman, infielders; Ducky Holmes and Huelsman, outfielders.

Before the season ended, left field had a new occupant in Jimmy Callahan, who had relinquished the managership to Fielder Jones in midsummer.

The new manager proved an ideal leader and the Sox, through a spurt at the close, waltzed into third place in the race, with Boston winning the championship. New York finished second, and after Chicago came Cleveland, Athletics, St. Louis, Detroit and Washington.

If any justification for the choice of Fielder Jones as manager was needed, the 1905 campaign, the season of preparedness for greater things, furnished it. With the exception of infielder Rohe, Jones practically stood pat on the team and made the race the most spectacular seen in the American League up to that time. For the greater part of the journey the White Sox and Athletics were neck and neck, Chicago leading in the middle of the season by a narrow margin. After falling behind when the season was two-thirds over, the Sox came again and by a sensational spurt came within one game of Connie Mack's whirlwinds. They played eleven games in six days away from home. The Sox lost, but they compelled the Athletics, the eventual winners, to travel the rocky road of uncertainty until the third from the last day of the season. At the finish the Athletics had won 92 games and lost 56; the Sox had won 92 and lost 60.

The rest of the contenders were outclassed, Detroit being the nearest, Boston, Cleveland, New York, Washington and St. Louis trailing.

Peace having been declared between the rival Chicago clubs, the post-season games were resumed. The brilliant playing of Frank Chance was a big factor in the victory of the Cubs, who vanquished the Sox four games out of five.

◆ CHAPTER XI ◆

The "Hitless Wonders" and Two Flags

Race in 1905 a curtain-raiser for greater things—Nineteen victories in a row—Sox win their third pennant—Defeat Cubs for the championship of the World—Charles W. Murphy is introduced—Gives his opinion of rival owner.

Comiskey's greatest year in baseball developed several changes from the 1905 lineup. George Rohe divided the third base position with Lee Tannehill, while Isbell became a second baseman. Callahan, having come to the conclusion that he could do better as a semi-pro magnate, quit the big ring, while Holmes and Danny Green were released. Dougherty, Hahn, O'Neill, Vinson, Hemphill, Fiene, Roth, Hart and Towne donned the white hosiery for the first time.

The fierceness of the struggle in 1905 had filled the home fans with the hope that the Sox would make a runaway race of it in 1906, but after a fair start the team was floundering in the unfamiliar surroundings of second division. In hitting they had, year after year, gradually dropped from .275 in 1901 to .237 in 1905. They had already acquired the title of "hitless wonders," but they were rapidly becoming more and more hitless without being wonders.

While the Sox were trying to get together, the Athletics, New York and Cleveland teams were having the race to themselves. Detroit threatened now and then. Sometimes the leaders were switched almost daily, but of the glory Chicago had no part.

Towards the latter part of July Fielder Jones had succeeded in getting his pitching staff in condition for a drive and, starting on August 2 he began his victory march of 19 straight games, a record surpassed but once in the history of baseball. Providence had won twenty straight in 1884, as a member of the National League, the pitching of "Hoss" Radbourne making the feat possible. As a unique feat in the annals of the game the complete record of the White Sox during this marvelous drive is here reproduced:

August 2—White Sox, 3; Boston, 0. White-Young.
August 3—White Sox, 4; Boston, 0. Walsh-Harris.
August 4—White Sox, 1; Boston, 0. Patterson-Dineen.
August 5—White Sox, 10; Athletics, 2. White-Bender.
August 6—White Sox, 7; Athletics, 2. Owen-Coombs, Coakley.
August 7—White Sox, 4; Athletics, 0. Walsh-Waddell.
August 8—white Sox, 1; Athletics, 0. Patterson-Plant (10 innings).
August 9—White Sox, 3; Athletics, 2. White-Dygert (10 innings).
August 10—White Sox, 2; New York, 1. Walsh-Chesbro.
August 11—White Sox, 8; New York, 1. Owen-Hogg, Newton, Chesbro.
August 12—White Sox, 3; New York, 0. Walsh-Orth.
August 13—White Sox, 0; New York, 0. White-Chesbro (9 innings).
August 15—White Sox, 6; Boston, 4. Walsh-Tannehill, Glaze.
August 16—White Sox, 9; Boston, 4. Patterson, Altrock-Harris.
August 17—White Sox, 4; Boston 3. Owen, White-Young.
August 18—White Sox, 10; New York, 0. Walsh-Chesbro.
August 20—White Sox, 4; New York, 1. White-Orth.
August 22—White Sox, 6; New York, 1. Walsh-Chesbro, Clarkson.
August 22—White Sox, 11; New York, 6. Owen-Hogg, Griffith.
August 23—White Sox, 4; Washington, 1. Patterson-Falkenberg.

The first twelve games were played at home. Then came three at Boston, four at New York and one at Washington.

It will be noticed that Walsh won seven of the nineteen games. His moist delivery was beginning its deadly work, which was repeated for six successive seasons. Walsh went up against some of the best pitchers in the league. Waddell, perhaps the greatest left-hander who ever lived, fared no better than the rest. Of this remarkable series eight games were shut-outs. Of these Walsh had four to his credit. The total number of runs the opposition garnered off of his delivery was six, fewer than one per game.

On August 7 the White Sox had reached second place in the race. On August 12 they looked down on the rest from the top. Once having reached the peak the real battle began and, still "hitless," but now "wonders," the White Sox won a reputation for gameness which has seldom been equalled. An indication of their pluck is furnished by the record of 29 games won during the season by one run.

On September 3 they were dislodged from first place by New York, the Highlanders holding the lead until the 13th. On September 14 Chicago was in a tie with New York, but they went to the front the next day. The Sox paled for just one day—September 21—but were back in the lead twenty-four hours later. Failing to stay down, the Gotham crew stepped over Comiskey's battling cohorts and took a front seat in the procession during September 23 and 24. Chicago, however, was through "fooling" and grabbed the lead on the 25th to hold it until the finish.

Putting any construction one pleases on the race as a whole, it was patent to any observer that the Sox had bluffed their way through. They finished with a team batting average of .228—the lowest in the league. Great pitching had been contributed by White, Walsh, Patterson and Owen, but runs are needed to win and gilt-edged twirling is often found among tailenders. The answer was found in strategy and team work. Given the slimmest kind of opening, a 100 percent defense would be necessary to keep the Sox from trundling the winning run over the plate. Their own defense was well nigh perfect.

On the offense the slogan was to get on the bases by hook or crook and to "claim everything." As a result no friendly greetings were exchanged between the manager and the umpires and before the season had come to a close Jones had worn a path between the plate and the bench.

Watching the maneuvers of the players while at home was an upstanding figure in a gray "bonnet." At every game he took his position behind the heavy wire screen under the stand. It wasn't the best place in the world for a lookout but it is not on record that any plays escaped him. Every forenoon the manager and the observer of the day before would meet in the private office of the president, a box-like stall close to the entrance and furnished with two chairs, a plain desk and a box of cigars.

The conversation would be brief and to the point. Jones would be apprised of the fact that the owner of the team had noticed a lot of things from behind the screen. Comiskey didn't believe much in "inside" baseball, but he did insist on his men playing the game "right." His principal strategy consisted in being in position to complete any play that might possibly come up. Nothing so exasperated him as a player failing to cover his base. Noticing once that second base had been left without a keeper after the ball had been hit he recalled this to the manager after the game.

"Tell the players," said Comiskey with some heat, "that they can get just as good a view of a ball going over the fence while standing on the bag as they can twenty feet away."

Comiskey has often been charged with interfering with his managers in running the team. Put to the test he probably would plead guilty. His pilots would also readily admit that they appreciated the interference from a man who had forgotten more baseball than most men knew. No one, however, ever accused "Commy" of coming between player and manager. When one from the ranks appeared in the "front office" it was either to get his pay check or the visit was at the suggestion of his field boss. If he had a kick when he came he left with the impression that he owed the universe an apology for being permitted to live.

With the 1906 pennant race over, preparations began for that classic combat between the Sox and the Cubs which, even to this day, is nurtured in song and story in the district "around the yards." The Cubs had captured the National League flag and had set a new record in games won with 116. The team was a worthy successor to Anson's "Heroic Legion" and boasted of an infield, which in some respects even surpassed that famed stonewall of the Eighties.

No greater combination had been seen for years than was offered by Chance, Evers, Tinker and Steinfeldt. In the outfield were Sheckard, Hofmann and Schulte. Brown, Overall, Ruelbach and Pfiester as pitchers had held the greatest batters in the National League in the hollow of their hands. Johnny Kling was rated as the top notch catcher and with Frank Chance as leader they were considered invincible by the West Side fans, the team going into the series heavy favorites.

Nick Altrock, who in 1903 had insisted that his stock in trade consisted of only his glove, won the first game for the Sox at the West Side park. The score was 2 to 1 and the South Side comedian went up against Mordecai Brown, then in his prime as a hurler. The second game was a walkover for the Cubs on the West Side grounds, Ruelbach, who opposed White, letting down the American leaguers with one hit, the score being 7 to 1.

The following day, on the West Side, George Rohe immortalized himself by pounding out a triple with the bases full, then and there winning the game, which ended 3 to 0. The Cubs could do nothing with Ed Walsh, who allowed but two hits. Jack Pfiester, for the losers, was almost as good, permitting four.

The Cubs evened up the series in the fourth game, through Brown's magnificent pitching, the three fingered wizard being hit safely only twice, the game winding up 1 to 0 in favor of the Nationals.

The fifth no-quarter contest, which went to the White Sox 8 to 6, was marked by Frank Isbell's four two-base hits. In the final White had the Cubs at his mercy, the Sox winning 8 to 3.

The result was an unexpected blow to the followers of the National League, but the defeat failed to affect the morale of the West Siders, who, in winning one pennant, acquired the habit.

The series between the Sox and the Cubs served to introduce Charles W. Murphy, who had purchased the Cubs before the championship season opened. As a coincidence his first title clash was with Charles A. Comiskey, whose fortunes he had followed when a cub reporter in Cincinnati. Having seen "Commy" play in his early days, and having been his rival for years, the following from Mr. Murphy's pen should be of peculiar interest:

> When I first knew Charles A. Comiskey, the beloved "Old Roman" of the famous Chicago White Sox, he was first baseman and manager of the time-honored Cincinnati team under Mr. Brush. I had located in Cincinnati after leaving my birthplace at Wilmington, Ohio, and was a "kid" reporter on the late John R. McLean's Cincinnati Enquirer. At that early age I was wild about baseball and never let an opportunity to see a game slide by. Harry Weldon was the sporting editor.
>
> After witnessing Comiskey play a few games I said one night to Weldon:

XI. The "Hitless Wonders" and Two Flags

"I wish I could have seen Commy play when he led the Browns to all those pennants over in St. Louis. I never saw anybody play such a deep first base and he seems to want everything that is coming from the umpire." "You are mighty right he does," replied Weldon, "because he knows that one bad decision may often lose the game and Comiskey is a hard loser. Why, the coaching box was invented to keep him away from the umpires. He was not what you would term an umpire baiter, but he spent plenty of time running up to the home plate when the umpires gave a particularly punk decision, which might turn victory into defeat."

Ever after that when I beheld the coaching box, as we see it today I usually associate it with Comiskey. When Comiskey managed the Reds he lived at the Grand Hotel in Cincinnati and was about the most popular man in the Queen City. It was then that I learned about what a magnetic personality he possessed. He was a chum of Col. Jerry Keirsted, Dr. Minor, Captain Tinker and other pioneer fans and they all loved him sincerely. After the ball game of evenings the crowd would gather around a big round table and play hearts. The ball game would also be played over in those reunions and I guess Comiskey could have been elected mayor at that time if he had aspired to a political career.

His great reputation had preceded him to Cincinnati and we all knew of his winning four flags in a row for St. Louis under Chris Von der Ahe. I thought before I saw Comiskey play that any stalwart player, who could bat, was acceptable as a guardian of the initial sack. Comiskey was the first player I ever saw who played so deep and allowed the pitcher to cover first base on many plays. He was a truly wonderful first baseman and really revolutionized the playing at that position, showing creative genius. Comiskey did not bat like Roger Conner, Dave Orr or Dan Brouthers, perhaps, but as an all-round first baseman he excelled sluggers of that type in his general worth to a club.

I doubt if there ever was a smarter player and his quick intuitive mind was well known in the baseball world. Comiskey has always been in sympathy with the players and that is one reason why he has been so successful in the national game.

I have always regarded Comiskey as the father of the American League and the sponsor of the president of that organization. There never has been any doubt in my mind that it was Comiskey who made the American League what it is today—the rival of the National League. His practical knowledge of baseball was known throughout the country and when he advised men with capital to become club-owners they listened to him and heeded his advice. It has always been my belief that Comiskey is the smartest man in baseball. His magnetic personality has had much to do in creating the wonderful loyalty to his great team on the South Side of Chicago.

He was my competitor for years for the patronage of the public and I always found him a fair fighter—never hitting below the belt. Few men in baseball realize the composite character of the "Old Roman"—his admirable mixture of sportsmanship with business acumen. To me he has always been more or less of an idol—a man to be looked up to. I formed a great admiration for "Commy" thirty years ago and it has increased each year since I met him. He was much admired by my sponsor in baseball, the late John T. Brush, who used to deplore that Comiskey was not in the National League. Today he is probably the greatest individual force in baseball and he has reached the present pinnacle by his own efforts solely. Comiskey would have been a success in any other line of human endeavor, because he is a go-getter. When he started his club in Chicago he took a long chance and shot at the moon—and hit it. Few men would have braved the hazardous investment in baseball as he did.

In time of chaos he is always cool and calm and his judgment is of the best. He knows the inherent strength of baseball

The White Sox of 1906, "The Hitless Wonders," world's champions. Upper row, left to right, Hart, E. McFarland, Davis, Comiskey, Isbell, Sullivan, White. Middle row: Walsh, Smith, Roth, Hahn, Dundon, Donohue, O'Neill, Tannehill, Rohe. Lower row: Towne, Altrock, Owen, Hallman, Dougherty, Jones, Fiene.

and its great hold on the American people. He realizes that it will always retain its popularity as long as it is kept clean and honest. My experience as a club-owner in Chicago has taught me to respect Comiskey's views on all subjects relating to baseball and I have noticed that when his advice is heeded in baseball policies, trouble of a serious nature is avoided. He knows how to feel the public pulse and is a great asset to the game. Long may he wave!

The ability of Comiskey as an organizer is best shown by the

> fact that until the American League was born no opposition could stand up against the National League. In the councils of the National League most of us regarded Comiskey as the brains of the American League. We always recognized his shrewdness and ability to do what the public liked.

With the Sox-Cubs series began the era of big money. The receipts set a record at $106,550. As the price of tickets averaged only a little over $1 the total did not reach the large figures of later years when admissions were inflated to two or three times the normal. This made the players' share of modest dimensions, so much so that when the pay checks were handed out, Comiskey presented to Manager Jones his share of the first four games—$15,000—to be distributed "among the boys."

♦ CHAPTER XII ♦

Two Pitch-Outs and a Mess of Bass

Long wait for a pennant—A season without a parallel—Sox lose bunting by one game—Fielder Jones resigns when partnership is denied—Joe Cantillon in need of friends—Comiskey moves into $1,000,000 plant—"Future Greats" join the team.

Having attained the peak in 1906, after a wait of twenty years, Comiskey was destined to run the cycle of eleven seasons before unfurling another pennant. In the interval five pilots tried their hand at getting the White Sox to the top. Four of them failed—a quartet from the major league school. It remained for a "busher," Clarence Rowland, to land the fourth American League flag for the "Old Roman."

Fielder Jones continued as manager until the close of the 1908 season. In each of the two years he drove the Sox into third place in the pennant race. In 1907 he finished five games behind Detroit, which beat out the Athletics by a nose, with Cleveland, New York, St. Louis, Boston and Washington trailing. Hard luck was the Sox portion all season. Injuries to Tannehill and Sullivan and mediocre work by Altrock and Patterson, two of the old reliables, put the world's best out of the running time and again, but in grit they were still champions, coming up smiling after each knockdown.

The same combination, which had won a world's title, made up the team, only minor changes being made. Armbruster was added to the catching staff and Hickman and Quillan to the infield.

The season of 1908 will stand without parallel in the annals of major league baseball. In each organization the pennant depended on the last game of the season with the striking coincidence added of the two Chicago teams figuring in both. In New York Merkle's lapse in failing to touch second base necessitated a play-off of the Cubs-Giants game the day after the season regularly closed. The victory of Chicago gave the Cubs their third straight flag.

In the West the White Sox and Detroit went into a clinch for the flag October 6, the final day of the schedule. The pennant would go to the winner as Cleveland, the third contender, had been eliminated by St. Louis a couple of days before. "Doc" White for the Sox, was knocked out of the box in the first inning, the Tigers scoring four runs. "Wild Bill" Donovan for Detroit was unhittable and Chicago failed to put a marker over the pan while Detroit added three for good measure.

While the dentist pitcher was sadly walking to the dugout "Iron Man" Walsh sallied forth. He had been on similar errands of mercy twenty times before during the season which, added to his regular journeys to the box, totaled 66, a record for the American League. In innings pitched it would figure up to 464. Having undergone the terrific strain of pitching in fourteen more than one-third of all the games in which the Sox had been engaged, he proved unequal to the task and was relieved by Frank Smith.

This erratic hurler held the Tigers at bay during the final innings of the game. If ever a pitcher had an opportunity to atone for his sins it was Smith. Even though finishing like a whirlwind,

Smith was held responsible for the loss of the pennant. The fans did not know. Comiskey and Jones did.

Two rash pitch-outs toward the middle of the season had deprived the White Sox of their fourth flag and a possible world's title. These pitch-outs were of minor consequence at the time. They loomed up as nothing else before or since, at the finish. Oddly enough, they had been made against the very team that eventually beat out the Sox in the last game of the season.

It happened at Detroit.

Smith was pitching.

At a critical stage he twice whizzed the ball wide of the plate on purpose. He figured that it was good strategy. No one else did. After the game Jones took the big twirler to task. Smith resented it and made a bluff of "going after the manager." Jones failed to report the occurrence to Comiskey on his return but the president heard of it. The episode brought out the "Old Roman's" idea of discipline in strong relief. He took the risk of losing a pennant in order to make an "example." Eventually it did cost him a flag or possibly two. A fortune went with it.

"What have you done to Smith?" was Comiskey's opening remark as he greeted his manager.

"Why, nothing," replied Jones, a little non-plussed.

"Well, why haven't you? I thought that you were the manager of the team."

"Am I?" queried the pilot.

"You have never been anything else and as long as you are with me you will remain so and I will back you up if you should suspend every man on the team for the balance of the season," said Comiskey.

"In that case Smith is laid off indefinitely," replied the manager.

"After you have broken the news to him send him to me," was the message from "Commy."

There is no stenographic report of the conference between owner and player, but Smith himself was authority for the statement that it was worth the season's suspension to listen to the "Old Roman."

Smith's justification of the two unlucky pitch-outs figured in the conversation as they did in the race. As he was not reinstated until the very end of the season, and this happened at the earnest solicitation of Jones, he, of course, had no opportunity of bolstering up the weakened pitching staff. As it turned out, had Smith won a single game the pennant would have flown at the Sox Park.

Realizing full well what the pitcher's defection had cost him Comiskey called Smith to his office after that disastrous final game with the Tigers. It was a shorter session than the first but equally impressive to the ball player.

"I told you once that you would not get a cent," said Comiskey. "I am going to keep my word. Here is a check for your full salary, but I am going to send it to your wife."

Smith had never recovered his speech since the initial interview, but he managed to blurt out, once on the outside:

"Take it from me, he's a square sport."

In that hectic game with the Tigers Jones finished his career as manager of the White Sox. As a player he was done with the sport forever, as he never faced another pitcher. Good-byes were said behind the screen as, true to his scrappy past, the umpires had ordered him off the field. Here he prophesied that the fans would vent their spleen on him for the disaster. It is a fact that they did and all because White had pitched in that first inning instead of Smith.

I sat under the stand with Jones from the time he was banished from the field to the end of the game.

"Why did I pick White?" he said in answer to a query. "I put him in because I figured him the best bet against the Tigers and because 'Doc' insisted. White had been a stumbling block for Detroit all season and he told me that he never felt better. The fans won't understand, though, and I will be 'panned' for fair."

That the criticism of the fans had something to do with the determination of Jones not to return to Chicago is certain, but there was a weightier reason why the South Siders saw him no more. It was not a question of salary. It was something bigger. Jones insisted on becoming a partner of Comiskey.

"Name your own terms and I'll give you a contract for as many years as you care to remain," was Comiskey's counter-proposal when Jones broached the question of partnership.

"A partnership or nothing," was the ultimatum of Jones and on that rock owner and manager split.

The relationship between Comiskey and his manager had been intimate and each had a high regard for the other. Both had been cast in the same mold as regards baseball—each being a superlatively hard loser. Both regarded the umpire as an objectionable appendage to the game. Neither could ever imagine an arbitrator with a friend during the playing season.

Joe Cantillon, manager of the Minneapolis American Association team, had been close to Comiskey for years but friendship ceased the minute Joe was appointed an umpire in the early days of the game. The fact that the two hunted and fished together for five months after the close of the season does not blunt the point to the story.

"I was umpiring in an important series between Baltimore and the Sox at the old Thirty-ninth street grounds," said Cantillon, in relating the incident. "The Sox got the short end of a few decisions on a Saturday and were defeated before a big crowd. On my way to the grounds on Sunday I ran into a couple of friends of mine who asked me to take them into the game. I told them I would try, although I figured that they would have a better chance if they applied themselves.

"Coming to the pass gate I asked the attendant to ask Comiskey, whom I saw standing in the distance, for a couple of tickets for my friends.

"'Sure,' he yelled so you could hear it out on the street, 'let him bring in all the friends he has. He will need them all today.'"

As they agreed about umpires, there came no harsh words from "Commy" when his manager started to wear a path between the plate and the bench. It was not long before Jones shared the dubious honor with Griffith, Comiskey's first manager, of being ordered off the field more often than anyone in the major leagues.

It was Jones who was indirectly responsible for one break between President Johnson and Comiskey, although he had no intention of being a party to the feud. It was during a tight race when Jones, after a run-in with the umpire, had been indefinitely suspended. Comiskey was hard up for players at this particular time and there was no one who could adequately substitute for the manager in center field. Coincident with the suspension Johnson sent a mess of bass to Comiskey.

"Does Ban want me to play the fish in the outfield?" asked Commy, and the big row was on.

That Comiskey could look beyond piscatorial differences became evident a couple of years later, and before a reconciliation between the two had been effected. Johnson was up for re-election as president of the league. Various suggestions were made regarding the length of term and salary attached to the office when Comiskey cut the debate short by making a motion that Johnson be elected for twenty years at $25,000 a year. With all that the owner of the White Sox never changed his opinion of Johnson's umpires.

XII. Two Pitch-Outs and a Mess of Bass

With the departure of Fielder Jones came an era of experiments. Catcher Billy Sullivan was appointed pilot of the White Sox for 1909. An effort had been made to bolster up the hitting strength of the team but without avail as, at the close of the season, it showed a team average of .221, four points below the percentage of the preceding year. Among those added to the team were Scott, Sutor and Olmstead, pitchers; Payne and Owens, catchers; Altizer, utility, and Messenger, Cravath, Cole, Welday and Barrows, outfielders.

Accidents became of daily occurrence. Jiggs Donohue failed at first. The terrific strain under which Walsh had worked began to tell on his iron constitution and he was far from effective. Smith, Scott and Sutor did good work but were unequal to the heavy burden and the team finished fourth, Detroit again winning, the Athletics and Boston coming next, while New York, Cleveland, St. Louis and Washington finished in the order named after Chicago.

The Cubs, having been temporarily flagged in the attempt to create a pennant trust, an opportunity was offered in the fall of 1909 for a city championship tilt. The Cubs nearly made a clean sweep, beating the Sox four out of five games.

Before the following spring Sullivan resigned and Hugh Duffy, Comiskey's former teammate in the Brotherhood, took charge and continued as leader for two years. The pitching department was strengthened by the signing of Young and Lange, the catching by Block, the infield by Gandil, McConnell, Zeider, Lord and Blackburne, and the outfield by the acquisition of Chouinard, John Collins, Zwilling, Browne and Meloan.

The gamble of the game was never better illustrated than by the release of Chick Gandil, which followed a disappointing trial. A few years later this player was to return and round out the championship team of 1917. Blackburne furnished another example. He was considered the star of the Eastern League and Comiskey paid

$11,000 for his release, a top figure at that time. Throwing his knee out of joint shortly after he had joined the Sox he became of little use to the team.

Worse luck pursued the team than in the previous year and the club was practically reorganized in midseason, with Sullivan's recovery from blood poisoning. Lord, McConnell and Blackburne were then added and towards the close of the season the shakeup began to yield returns. Despite the lowest team batting of which a major league aggregation has ever been guilty—.212—the Sox finished sixth to the Athletics, with New York second, Detroit third, Boston fourth, Cleveland fifth, Washington seventh and St. Louis last.

The lowly standing of the Sox did not correspond to their environment at the end of the season. During the year they had moved from the modest home on Thirty-ninth street to Thirty-fifth street and Shields avenue, where Comiskey had built the greatest ball park in the land. Grand stand and bleacher were of concrete and steel and were arranged to seat 28,500. Later these were enlarged to take care of 32,000, which was the capacity at the world's series games in 1917. Surrounding the entire field is an ornamental brick wall. Only one field in the country exceeds it in size, the Boston National League park, which is deeper. The Polo Grounds in New York has the depth but lacks the distance in right and left fields.

The cost of the park measured Comiskey's wealth at the time, which was well over the half-million mark. To-day the plant could not be duplicated for less than $1,000,000. Time and again when it was suggested that improvements at the old grounds would be appreciated Comiskey would always reply that as soon as he could pay cash for land and stands he would build a park which would be a monument to the game. He made good his word when the new park was thrown open on July 1.

For a long time he had had his eye on the property on the site of the old Brotherhood grounds at 35th street and Wentworth avenue. When opportunity offered he closed the deal but on account of a clause in the lease he was unable to get control at the time of the actual spot on which the big revolt of 1890 had been staged. Consequently he was compelled to go several hundred feet further west than had been his original intention.

It was no idle figure of speech when he announced that the new home of the Sox was dedicated to the fans. Most everybody took him at his word and thousands have appropriated a share since then. Seldom have the gates been closed. The feet of thousands have trampled on the grass, which never had a chance to grow up. Church festivals, barbecues, free lance games, meets of all descriptions, picnics and fairs have had their turn at "Commy's Park." On the walls of his office hang engraved testimonials to his generosity, but none tells the anguish of ground keepers or gives a hint at the fortunes spent in making the field fit for the regular games.

Some years ago "auto polo" became the rage. Some of Comiskey's friends were interested in its promotion. Could they have the use of the field? Certainly, and "use" it they did. Up in the stand sat Comiskey watching the two contesting cars chop his field into ribbons. It cost him $400 to repair the damage. When it was over he set up a "feed" to everybody who wished to partake of it and he never charged a cent for the use of the grounds.

"Why do you permit every Tom, Dick and Harry to use your field?" asked a fellow magnate once.

"How could I refuse?" queried the "Old Roman." "The fans built the park, didn't they?"

It is this attitude which explains the loyalty of the White Sox fan. Win or lose it is all the same. They know that whatever the circumstances they will get a square deal. When Comiskey first ordered the covered stand thrown open to his bleacher patrons on rainy days

This is the White Sox team of 1917, champions of the American League and winners over the New York Giants for the world's title. In the center and forefront is Manager Rowland. Behind him to the right stands Kid Gleason, then coach now manager. With the exception of Dick Kerr and a number of utility players and late-comers, the group includes every member of the 1919 team—the combination that the Old Roman has pronounced the greatest he has ever owned or managed. In front are those old mainstays, Claude Williams, Joe Jackson, Chick Gandill, Ray Schalk, Eddie Collins, Eddie Cicotte, Nemo Leibold and Buck Weaver, who have done so much to keep the white hose spotless. The inserts, reading from left to right, are: Harry Grabiner, secretary; Mr. Comiskey, owner, and Lou Comiskey, treasurer. The eastern wing of the mammoth White Sox grandstand serves as background.

there were a few complaints from those who had invested in the more expensive seats.

"Well, I don't think the majority sit in the bleachers from choice," parried Comiskey. "Baseball has grown, but the pocketbooks of some of our patrons have not. As I can't get them all in my office I have to do the best I can to keep them from getting wet."

Depending on his employees to look after the comfort of the fans in the stands he himself took charge of the entertainment indoors. Over the half-dozen entrances leading into the grand stand he built his offices and reception rooms. The Woodland Bards' room is the center of the latter. Here gather the members of this exclusive organization which now consists of several hundred, to gaze on the trophies of the chase and the rod. In addition there are priceless mementoes of the ball field—gifts from the great of the earth, prized souvenirs collected from every part of the world. Open house, with the good things of life on tap, is kept 365 days in the year. There is not a country on earth which has not had its representatives inside its four walls.

Newcomers always insist on seeing "Commy." For everybody there is a "feel at home" greeting. The visitor leaves with the impression that he has known the "Old Roman" all his life.

"How can you stand being slapped on the back all day long?" was asked of Comiskey.

"The minute they stop I want to die," was his answer, and it was not said in the spirit of self-adulation, either. "There is nothing I enjoy more than to see others enjoy themselves. When the gang quits I am through."

The more aristocratic surroundings seemed to influence the team in nobler deeds in 1911, and it finished fourth with the Athletics again winners. Detroit and Cleveland wound up in second and third place, respectively, while Boston was fifth, New York sixth, Washington seventh and St. Louis eighth.

The changes in the lineup had been slight, the more important being the addition of Kreitz to the catching staff, Mullin and Corhan to the infield, Ping Bodie (Pizzola) and McIntyre to the outfield and the return of Jimmy Callahan, who went to left field.

The new talent boosted the team batting to a higher point than it had been in ten years. McIntyre and Lord brought up the average and Bodie, who came with a high reputation from the Pacific Coast League, did his part, but did not quite come up to expectations.

Comiskey had high hopes of Bodie, especially after it had cost him $10 for an introduction. The Sox trained at Mineral Wells that spring. "Commy" was sitting in the lobby of the hotel, talking with friends, when the robust Californian hove to in front of him.

"Could you stand for a $10 advance, Commy?" asked the massive athlete.

"Sure," answered the Sox owner. "Tell White (manager of the rookies) to give you the money."

"Who was he?" someone asked.

"I haven't met him socially yet," answered the Sox boss, "but I saw him put the ball over the fence yesterday and I'll stand a tap for anybody that can do that."

It was not unusual for Comiskey not to know half of the rookies that appeared in the spring. In the anxiety to get a winning team he purchased them practically by the carload. If one or two made good out of the lot he considered he had made a good investment.

Not being able to pick them out himself he trusted to others to see that they showed up with at least the normal number of legs and arms. Frequently, however, he got bit. Not many years ago he signed a player, touted as a wonder by an Iowa manager. When he reported Comiskey discovered that it was possible to sneak up on him on his blind side as he had only one eye.

Although his bunch of recruits failed to furnish any major league talent the Sox were kept fairly well to the front by the great work of Ed Walsh. When the time rolled around for the annual set-to with the Cubs the ball he served up was again cutting strange capers. Mainly through the "Iron Man's" pitching the Sox made a clean sweep, winning four games in a row. Walsh figured in three. He won the first and fourth and finished the second. Adding the three to his season's record he had participated in 58 games since spring.

XII. Two Pitch-Outs and a Mess of Bass

Jimmy Callahan returned to the managership in 1912 and he remained as pilot until the close of the 1914 season. With the switch came a search for baseball talent. The net was spread the country over and when the season closed the following newcomers had figured on the pay roll: Peters, Cicotte, Benz, Delhi, Jordan, Bell and Taylor, pitchers; Kuhn, Easterly and Schalk, catchers; Borton, Fournier, Johnson, Weaver, Paddock, Ens and Rath, infielders, and Mattick, outfielder.

During the final games the battery of Cicotte and Schalk was paraded before the fans, a pair destined to become headliners in Comiskey's capture of his fourth American league pennant and his third world's flag. Both were of the "Wee Willie" type. Cicotte, the pitcher, was rated as a veteran. The catcher was not old enough to vote. The Boston American League contributed Cicotte. The Milwaukee American Association turned over Ray Schalk for a cash consideration of $18,000.

Schalk appeared on the Sox field towards the end of the season. His first job was to warm up Ed Walsh in pitching practice. The big fellow, whom doting fans had nicknamed the "Big Moose," sized up the youngster behind the plate and felt compassion in his soul. He motioned to him.

"You have probably heard that I throw a ball hard to catch," warned Walsh. "There is also some speed behind it but I'll just ease 'em in. I don't want to queer you."

Schalk thanked him but expressed curiosity as to how speedy he could hand them up. It was tradition that Walsh's neck assumed a carmine tint in proportion to his physical effort. He never left the box with a more ruddy sunset above his collar than he did after that warm-up. High and low, in and out, they came, spitter, curve and straight. All looked alike to the pygmy back stop, who acted as if he was suffering from ennui.

Walsh did not discuss further his cannon-ball delivery but he suggested to Callahan that he would like to have the diminutive catcher as battery mate for the rest of the season. As a matter of fact, despite his terrific speed, Schalk always insisted that Walsh was one of the easiest of pitchers to catch. On the other hand he has contended that Urban Faber throws one of the "heaviest" balls ever handled although the latter does not use as fast a delivery as did Walsh.

Another player who came to the front in 1912 was Buck Weaver, the firebrand of the team. Buck had been brought from the Pacific Coast, where he had nearly set a record for errors, having accumulated 70 in 132 games, while playing the infield.

The three—Cicotte, Schalk and Weaver—formed a nucleus for the world's champions of 1917, but they were unable to do more than to lend a helping hand for a fourth place position in the 1912 pennant race. Boston captured the flag. Washington and Philadelphia were next, while following Chicago were Cleveland, Detroit, St. Louis and New York.

With the regular season over the Cubs and Sox went into a clinch for the annual Chicago title series. It took nine games to decide the winner. The first two were ties. The next three were won by the Nationals and then followed an exhibition of gameness seldom equalled, the Sox winning four in a row and adding another banner to its collection.

With the curtain rung down the mighty Ed Walsh practically faded from view. He had figured in 62 games during the season, within four of the mark which he set in 1908. He dropped to 16 in 1913, another year of additions to the Sox, but with a lower standing in the race. Fifth was the best they could get, while ahead of them were the Athletics, Washington, Cleveland and Boston, with Detroit, New York and St. Louis bringing up the rear.

Among the newcomers on the team had been O'Brien and

Russell, pitchers; Chase and Berger, infielders; Chapelle, Beall and Schaller, outfielders.

Chapelle figured in the second $18,000 deal between Comiskey and the Milwaukee team. He had been the fence buster in the American Association but failed to deliver for Chicago. This was, however, partly due to an injury sustained in the spring.

As a matter of form the Sox and Cubs went to grips for the city championship in the fall, the American Leaguers winning four out of six games. With the series concluded Comiskey and Callahan made haste to prepare for the historic trip around the world.

Late to get under way for the 1914 season, the Sox failed to "arrive," winding up in seventh place in the pennant race in one of the most disastrous campaigns in which a Comiskey team has ever participated. Leading Chicago to the wire were the Athletics, Boston, Washington, Detroit, St. Louis and New York. Cleveland finished below the Sox.

New names on the roster were Breton, Alcock and Baker, infielders; Demmitt, Roth and Daly, outfielders; Mayer, catcher, and Lathrop, Faber and Wolfgang, pitchers.

Despite their lowly standing the Sox again defeated the Cubs in the city series, four games to three.

♦ CHAPTER XIII ♦

Purse Strings Are Untied

Clarence Rowland at the helm—Collins and Jackson make Comiskey poorer by $130,500—Two years without poker—Story of the Federal League war—Charles Weeghman "sits in"—Sox win American League pennant—Whip the New York Giants for the world's title.

Comiskey entered upon a new era in baseball just prior to the season of 1915. He went to the "sticks" for a manager and to the majors for players, completely reversing his policy of former years. In Dubuque, Iowa, he dug up Clarence H. Rowland, who in the previous season had piloted the Peoria team of the "Three I" League. Jimmy Callahan, disappointed over the showing of the team, had resigned, and the "busher" took the helm. In three years, aided by an unlimited bank roll, he was destined to win a pennant and a world's championship for the man who discovered him.

Up to this time Comiskey had spent more for minor league players than both of his ball parks had cost him. Few had made good. With the change of administration he decided to take another tack. He would go after the finished product. Coincident with this resolution Connie Mack of the Philadelphia Athletics was meditating the breaking up of his famous combination of pennant winners. Comiskey heard of it and acted. Catching a fast train for the east, in company with Ban Johnson, he closed the deal for Eddie Collins, sensational second baseman of Mack's team.

The transaction set a record. Before Comiskey had succeeded in signing the keystone star, who had doubled in baseball and logic at the Columbia University, his bank account had been reduced to the extent of $65,000. Connie Mack received $50,000 and Collins was given a bonus of $15,000 for attaching his signature to a five-year contract which called for $15,000 a year.

Later in the season, with the Cleveland club in the hands of the bankers, "Commy" sent his secretary, Harry Grabiner, to the Forest City with instructions to buy Jackson, to fame known as "sockless Joe," and one of the leading hitters in the league.

"How far will you go?" asked Grabiner as he was handed the signed but otherwise blank check.

"The blank space is for you to fill in," was Comiskey's response.

Jackson was signed. The men who had the club in charge were given a check for $31,500 and an option on three players. After this had been exercised the Sox owner scratched from his books Chappelle, who had cost him $18,000; Bobby Roth, who stood him $11,000, and Edward Klepfer, originally bought for $5,000. The total made $65,500, and another new record had been set.

Having plugged up his infield and outfield with major league talent Comiskey took a $12,000 journey into the minor leagues. In the American Association a Milwaukee youth by the name of Felsch, christened "Happy" by the fans on account of his sunny disposition, had been burning up the league with his hitting and outfielding.

"How much?" wire Comiskey to the owners in Milwaukee.

"You may have him for $12,000," came the answer.

Comiskey hauled out his check book and Felsch became a member of the White Sox. He immediately proceeded to set the American League on fire as he had scorched the Association. He was not in Speaker's, Cobb's or Jackson's class as a hitter at the start but he could show each some pointers on how to field. Throwing the ball like a rifle shot unerringly from deep center to the plate without being set for the heave was one of his accomplishments and many maintain that as a center fielder he has no superior.

Although Felsch had few weaknesses on the ball field he had a failing while in civilian attire. "Happy" insisted in staying in every pot in the royal game of draw, a procedure which tended to a wide distribution of the contents of his pay envelope twice a month. Manager Rowland concluded that continually drawing two cards to a flush or repeated efforts to fill inside straights would, in time, cloud his sunny disposition, and he shut down on the game. For two years the White Sox went pokerless, except for a brief interval, a predicament in which no club had ever found itself before or probably since.

Managerial dictum having banished the pasteboards temporarily the players themselves, shortly afterwards, made the unusual departure from established customs permanent. Rowland had reinstated the 25-cent limit game after he had exacted a promise from Felsch that the latter would be more circumspect in calling for cards, but the life of the game was limited to half a dozen sessions. Buck Weaver had a bad evening, dealt some harsh comments along with the cards, remembered them the next day and came to the conclusion that the indoor pastime might affect his playing outdoors. The morning following Buck came to the manager with this proposal:

"If you see me in another game of poker before August 1 fine me $100."

"That goes for me, too," echoed half a dozen others.

With the period of grace up the Sox were in the thick of the pennant fight and as no one started to shuffle the cards the ban held for the balance of the season. An exception should be noted, however. A regular game was always going on in the rear of the Pullman when the team was on the road. It went under the term of "paresis" with the deuces and joker wild and the players twice as riotous. Eddie Collins was the "banker" and the stakes sometimes went as high as a dime if somebody raised the plunger who opened it.

Nemo Liebold was separated from the Cleveland club during the 1915 season by Comiskey. Nemo, besides being a hard man to pitch to, was the fortunate possessor of a "baby stare" in the indoor pastime, a great asset while the game lasted. Eddie Murphy pried himself loose from Connie Mack's slipping champions in order to have the privilege of sitting in with his former teammate, Eddie Collins. Add Quinlan, Johns and Brief and the recruits are accounted for.

Inability to get an even break in the series with Boston, Detroit and Washington during the season put the White Sox in third place despite the outlay of over $150,000 for players. Boston and Detroit finished ahead of the Sox, while Washington, New York, St. Louis, Cleveland and the Athletics trailed.

In the fall series with the Cubs the Sox, as had become their habit, won easily, capturing four out of five games. With the final game the West Side Ball Park ceased to be a battle ground for the two rival teams. During the following winter Charles W. Murphy sold the Cubs to Charles H. Weeghman, who combined them with his Federal League team, thus bringing to a close the experiment of trisecting Chicago's baseball map. The North Side now became the permanent home of the new Cubs.

Mr. Weeghman, who succeeded Mr. Murphy as president of the club, was a Chicago business man, fan and good fellow, and had been one of the principal figures in the Federal League war which raged during 1914 and 1915. As the "outlaw" league had but little influence on the fortunes of the White Sox only a brief outline of its history will be given in these pages.

The league was founded on the theory that "money will make the mare go." Its promoters originated the perambulating bank which consisted of a satchel crammed with $1,000 bills. It was carried around the country guarded by Jim Gilmore, president of the league, John B. Ward of Brooklyn, Phil Ball of St. Louis and Charles H. Weeghman of Chicago. Whenever a draft on major league talent was made the satchel would be opened and the contents would be dumped in the center of a table. If this did not make an impression on the player the promoters took the next train.

Fabulous salaries were offered. Some were accepted. Walter Johnson, under contract to the Washington club of the American League, was tendered a three-year contract by President Weeghman at $20,000 a year. Ty Cobb, Tris Speaker and others were offered as much. Speaker, who was a member of the Comiskey-McGraw world tour party, was apprised of his good fortune through a cablegram which finally caught up with him at Paris. Through an accident the message fell into the hands of John McGraw and the cat was out of the bag. The cables sizzled back and forth. The Giants' manager conferred with Comiskey. The latter refused to get excited.

"I don't see why I should interfere," asserted the "Old Roman." "If there is a bunch of men who wants to lose a lot of money in baseball it is none of my business. My club will be in California training camp on the scheduled date and I expect that most of the players will show up as usual."

Comiskey's prediction came true. Not a single regular player jumped the White Sox for the Federals. They all reported on time. Afterwards it turned out that a secret agreement had been made not to "monkey" with Commy's players.

"The man who whipped the National League should be let alone," was the advice of President Gilmore.

This, however, did not prevent the "Fed" magnates from having a reception committee of their own when the Lusitania arrived in New York with the tourists. The rivalry of organized and unorganized baseball owners to get in touch with the players on board assumed an opéra bouffe character. Each feared for the "evil" counsel of the other. Both were equally anxious to set the player "right" as to the real situation. All tried to reach the ship at quarantine. The organized baseball forces won and plowed their way through a snow storm on a revenue cutter to the big liner. This maneuver postponed the opening of the "satchel" until the players landed.

The pickings from the world tour bunch was comparatively small as only four out of twenty-three players joined the third league.

The raid for the rest of the season was confined mostly to the National League. When it came to territory, there was opposition in only two American League cities while the National had to contend against four rival clubs. Chicago, St. Louis, Pittsburgh and Brooklyn were the major league cities invaded. Indianapolis, Baltimore, Buffalo and Kansas City made up the rest of the circuit. Indianapolis, which had also won the pennant in a much restricted Federal League circuit in 1913, captured the flag in 1914. Chicago was second.

The only cities in which the Federals actually built for the future were Chicago and Brooklyn. In each steel and concrete stands were erected and the plants compared favorably with the best in the land.

The fight was continued during the season of 1915, in which year Chicago carried off the pennant. President Gilmore dug up more and more "millionaires" and the contents of the satchel were always in the center of the table. In the heat of the battle, during the middle of the season, it was decided to sign some of Comiskey's players. The effort proved a complete failure. The players stuck to the "Old Roman." Before the end of the season came overtures for

"Commy"

The first real present for the Sox fans was Eddie Collins. Miss South Side is proudly toting the $50,000 beauty home, led by the Old Roman. Cartoonist Sidney Smith gives a hint of other gifts to follow in the armful of packages carried by "Commy." He guessed rightly. Joe Jackson was among them.

peace. At its close a peace agreement was reached, the major leagues taking over the players and certain properties of the Federal.

The experiment of a third league proved a colossal failure. The losses incurred by all three organizations were enormous. It was claimed that John B. Ward had put nearly $700,000 into the Federal venture. Others contributed in proportion to their wealth or enthusiasm for the cause. The losses of organized baseball consisted mostly in a lessened attendance, defection of players and the obligations assumed at the settlement.

Prior to the peace agreement the Federal League had entered suit against the two major leagues which was heard by Judge Kenesaw Mountain Landis, in the Federal Court at Chicago. The fight was made principally on the "reserve clause," a rule which bound the player to a particular club, until released. Decision was never rendered, Judge Landis at various times hinting that if he should be compelled to cut the Gordian knot the entire baseball structure would crumble.

It was during the hearing that Judge Landis handed down the opinion that baseball must be regarded as a "national institution."

No player from his club having jumped during the hostilities Comiskey did not profit by the return of the prodigals when the agreement was signed and at the beginning of the 1916 season two infield positions were still "vacant." Jack Ness, Fred McMullin and Zeb Terry were signed to try for them. Claude Williams and Dave Danforth were added to the pitching staff, while the veteran John Lapp became change catcher.

Principally due to Eddie Cicotte's wonderful work in the box the team landed in second place after a terrific battle with Boston clear down to the wire, with Detroit only a few points behind. Below the Tigers were New York, St. Louis, Cleveland, Washington and Philadelphia in order named.

Although the Cubs had changed owners their luck had not and the fall series with the White Sox was a mere formality, the Americans winning four straight games.

The race in 1916 had been close enough to give the fans a foretaste of what was coming, and the followers of the Sox were vociferous but not surprised when Comiskey, after a wait of eleven years, "arrived" in 1917. It was his fourth flag in the American League. When he defeated the New York Giants he hung up his third world's championship emblem.

The Sox had had a hard fight in their own league and were pursued by Boston clear to the end. Nearest to the Red Sox were Cleveland, Detroit, Washington, New York, St. Louis and Philadelphia in order.

Beginning the 1917 season Comiskey, having tried ever since the release of Jiggs Donohue to plug the hole at first base, eventually succeeded, and Chick Gandil, purchased from Cleveland, at last rounded out the team. Eddie Cicotte's phenomenal pitching did the rest and the team finished with 100 games won and 54 lost. Charles Risberg was added to the infield and Byrd Lynn to the catching staff.

Envious rivals insisted that the White Sox rode to the front on Cicotte's mysterious "shine ball," a delivery which blinded some of the greatest sluggers in the league. The "jump ball" of Dave Danforth also served to clutter up President Johnson's desk with horsehide exhibits. Protests, strategy boards and chemical analysis, all failed and the riddle remains unsolved.

With the flag clinched the Sox were primed for the grand windup. The Giants had ridden rough shod over the rest of the contenders in the National League and had won the bunting in their own organization with a trifle greater ease than had Chicago. John McGraw, Comiskey's world-tour partner, was in command of New

York's best. It was the Napoleon of the game against the "busher" and fortune favored the "unknown."

Six games, equally divided between mediocrity and brilliancy, were played, and of these the White Sox won four. The first two were played in Chicago. The home club won both, by the scores of 2 to 1 and 7 to 2.

Brilliant pitching by Rube Benton helped to shut out the White Sox 2 to 0 in the first game at New York. Schupp repeated in the second, on the same field, the Giants winning 5 to 0, and the series stood at evens. Chicago took the next at home 8 to 5 and clinched the championship by annexing the sixth and last contest on the Polo Grounds, by the score of 4 to 2.

Featuring newspaper "leads" the morning after the final game, was the thrilling narrative of a footrace between Heinie Zimmerman and Eddie Collins, a sprint which practically decided the winner. It happened in Chicago's half of the fourth inning. Zimmerman, playing third base for New York, made a wild throw to first on Collins and the Chicago captain reached second. Joe Jackson lifted a fly to Robertson, who dropped the ball, and Collins ran to third.

When Felsch hit to Pitcher Benton, Collins purposely made a bluff at going home. Benton, observing the maneuver, ran towards the third base line to turn Collins back, eventually throwing to Zimmerman. Catcher Rariden, in the meantime, had run up the line leaving the plate unprotected. Collins, sizing up the prospects, darted towards home. Zimmerman was now in the unenviable fix of being unable to let go of the ball as he had no one to throw it to. It was up to him to tag Eddie. His lack of speed, as the $50,000 beauty romped home, furnished the material for the ditty, "You can't catch me, Heinie Zim."

Fate has set apart a "goat" in every world's series. Zimmerman became the burden bearer in the 1917 title clash, but undeservedly so. Critics, after a second sober thought, could devise no strategy which would have relieved Heinie of the responsibility which had been thrust upon him by others.

If artistically the games fell below par the financial returns were on a scale which had been exceeded but once before—the Boston-New York series of 1912. The side embellishments ranged from baked muskies to special trains. Of the latter Comiskey had five, two for the rooters to and from New York for the third and fourth games and three for players and newspaper men on each trip between the two cities.

The receipts for the six games were $425,000. Comiskey's share was in the neighborhood of $100,000. In 1885, in his first world's series experiment the total taken in at the gates amounted to $2,000, but he enjoyed his portion a great deal more than he did thirty-two years later. There were no ticket problems and no scalpers in those days.

After the series Comiskey was a candidate for the sanitarium. Approximately 200,000 clamored for the privilege of buying tickets for the first game. There were only 32,000 seats.

With the Sox the world's champions the fans, of course, forgot all about their inability to get the requisite number of pasteboards. They started rooting for next season the minute the last ball had been pitched. They would have done the same had their favorites lost. I happened to be at the Sox Park a few days after the series had ended. A "hey there," from outside brought the office force to the windows fronting on Thirty-fifth street. A coal wagon had been halted.

"Joe Jackson coming back next season?" shouted the grimy charioteer.

"Sure."

"And Ci-cot-tee?"

"Certainly."

"Great. The boys around the yard wanted to know? Giddap," and the horses disappeared under the viaduct.

Shot to pieces by enlistments and drafts the White Sox failed to make any kind of showing during the season of 1918. After a bumpy race they finished sixth, Boston winning the pennant with Cleveland, Washington, New York and St. Louis ahead of the Sox in order named, Detroit and Philadelphia alone barring the way to the cellar. Owing to the frequent departure of players no real effort could be made to plug up the holes and of the dozen recruits signed only one or two came up to the mark.

With the opening of the 1919 season a new manager was given command of the White Sox. Clarence Rowland had become a stockholder in the Milwaukee American Association club and "Kid" Gleason, who had with the exception of one season acted as coach since 1912, took charge. Gleason is of the old school of baseball but is not the "Kid" of the former St. Louis Browns. The Sox manager started in as a pitcher and later became a star infielder.

Gleason is the optimist among managers and possesses the faculty of being a Simon Legree without the players finding out about it. His admirable personal traits, rugged honesty and aggressive tactics have made him one of the most popular leaders the Sox ever had.

Early in the season of 1919 the White Sox, under the brilliant leadership of Gleason, took their rightful place in the sun. They forged to the front and stayed there. They ceased to be the "hitless wonders" and became the hitting terrors of the league. In team batting they passed the .280 mark on different occasions, leading the league practically throughout the season. Their defensive work was equally as brilliant, the team being near the front row most of the time.

The feat of acting as pacemakers for the greater part of the season was enough to set them apart from other combinations, past or present. As a fighting aggregation they were in a class by themselves. Coming from behind and winning became a habit.

The players who found their stride after the disastrous 1918 season were familiar to the Sox fans. The old faces were back. Most of the new ones decorated the bench. Pitcher Richard Kerr was the exception. This sterling twirler, bought from the Milwaukee American Association team, did yeoman service for a pitching staff which had been counted woefully weak but which, at the finish, held its own against all comers. Cicotte "repeated." Claude Williams came back. Later on were added the veterans George Lowdermilk, Erskine Mayer and Bill James. Urban Faber had a hard time getting in condition. Benz, Russell and Shellenback were missing.

Schalk did the catching and rang up a record of catching in 100 games per year in six consecutive years. The playing of Gandil, E. Collins, Weaver, McMullin and Risberg in the infield was the sensation of the league. Equally brilliant were the performances of Jackson, Felsch, Liebold and John Collins in the outfield.

Comiskey watched the team month after month and near the waning of the season could say that the White Sox were then the greatest team he ever had anything to do with.

"It is a wonderful combination—the greatest team I ever had," he said. "I can't pick out individuals because they are all giants in baseball. It is by all odds the greatest team in the American League. I couldn't pass a higher compliment. I can afford to single out one, Kid Gleason, because he is a manager. He has kept pace with the team and that means something.

"It is the best bunch of fighters I ever saw. No game is lost until the last man is out. They can think for themselves which is still better. To say that I am proud of them is putting it mildly. They have been setting the pace most of the time and no other team deserves being in front more than they."

♦ CHAPTER XIV ♦

Dig Spikes in Five Continents

Comiskey and McGraw start on a long journey—Many lands get a glimpse of the Sox and Giants—World's tour consumes 142 days—High jinks on the sea—Nation's great in the receiving line—Hard task is assigned Statue of Liberty.

While winning championships for Chris von der Ahe, Comiskey had dreamed of touring the world with a baseball team. When A. G. Spalding anticipated him in 1888 the manager of the Browns was disappointed but not broken-hearted. He would bide his time, but then and there he decided that he would head his own team when the omens were propitious for the journey. He had been one of the first to get an invitation from Spalding but Von der Ahe objected and "Commy" stayed at home.

Fortune having smiled on his undertakings he was ready to start in 1913. He had contemplated an earlier getaway. In fact the trip was the consummation of seven years of preparation. Immediately after winning the world's championship in 1906 "Commy" had announced that a world's tour was the next thing on the program. All he needed was a partner. It took him seven years to get one. Financial considerations had not figured, as the White Sox owner had let it be known that he would assume all the responsibilities. This he didn't have to do, as John McGraw, manager of the Giants, had persuaded the owners of the New York club to permit him to "borrow" the team for a trip.

It has been erroneously stated that the stockholders of the Gotham club backed McGraw. Nothing is farther from the truth. John McGraw took all the risk himself and it meant pledging his entire fortune. McGraw knew nothing about the intention of Comiskey to bear all the losses, if any, for both teams. His gameness, however, was appreciated and by none more than Comiskey.

The plans for the journey were perfected during the summer of 1913, and advance agents sent on ahead. The arrangements included special trains and other specialties. The best hotel accommodations that could be obtained were contracted for the world around. The sky was the limit and long before the season was over the obligations assumed approached the $100,000 mark. Solicitous friends of both promoters became anxious. Experienced globe trotters were free with their advice. A fortune would be lost if the elaborate plans were persisted in.

"Too bad I wasn't told that before I handed the steamship company my check for $90,000," said Comiskey with a smile.

To make certain that he would have enough for emergencies the "Old Roman" bought a letter of credit for 25,000 pounds sterling, approximately $121,000. McGraw carried a more modest account, but at that ample for all contingencies.

The interval between the departures of the first and second world tourists measured twenty-five years, lacking a day. Spalding and his party headed through the Golden Gate Nov. 18, 1888; Comiskey and McGraw with their White Sox and Giants, sailed from Seattle Nov. 19, 1913. Japan, China and the Philippines had been outside the itinerary of the original globe trotters. The twentieth century tourists were to exhibit before the little brown men of the Mikado's kingdom, the almond-eyed celestials and before the reformed head hunters of Uncle Sam's island possessions. They would not get a glimpse of Mauna Loa nor get a chance to entertain the Maoris of New Zealand, but to make up for these geographical misses, America's national game would be expounded to Nipponese and Chinese, Moro and Hindu.

Differing from the first world tour, there was no uncertainty as to the lanes to be followed. The first travelers had originally contemplated only a trip to the Antipodes. It was not until the party reached Australia that it was determined to complete the circle.

Comiskey and McGraw had mapped out every foot of the journey weeks before they left Chicago. They never deviated a hair's breadth from the schedule with the exception of cutting their stay in Japan short three days, due to failure of the ship to arrive on time. There were round-the-world tickets for 67 people in the hands of the secretaries at the start. One of these had seen enough salt water on the way to Yokohama and decided to stick to land as much as possible. Taking the overland trip through Siberia he met the party at Naples three months later. Another one was originally booked only as far as Japan and this left 66 for the "round trip."

The two trips were also dissimilar in another important respect aside from the route followed. While the primary reason for Spalding's jaunt was to introduce baseball to the benign in foreign lands, advantage was taken of the opportunity to show the superiority of America's sporting goods. There was nothing reprehensible in this, but the commercial touch marked the contrast. Comiskey and McGraw made their pilgrimage distinctly a "sporting" proposition.

Perhaps the disinterested motives influenced the great of the earth to treat the visitors as official emissaries of the great American republic. Thus the "Old Roman" and his partner were congratulated on their enterprise and on the game by the highest in the Mikado's government. Shanghai and Hongkong gave them their best. The keys of Manila were theirs. Lord Denman, governor general of Australia, not only entertained the pilgrims in his official mansion, but in addition was initiated into the mysteries of the curve. The Khedive of Egypt personally thanked "Commy" and McGraw for their visit to the land of the Sphinx. The Italian government was equally solicitous as was the French, which turned over the nationally owned Longchamps race track in Paris for the game, which, however, was not played.

As a climax to ovations which belted the globe came verbal congratulations from the head of the greatest empire on earth, King George V of England, after he had witnessed a sensational eleven-inning game in London.

Aside from national recognition there was not a city or state visited which was not lavish in its hospitality. Dennison, Texas, stayed up nearly all night for a chance to entertain the tourists; Osaka, Japan, bestirred itself at dawn in order to show its appreciation. Receptions and banquets followed each other with bewildering frequency and eight months' training alone saved the athletes from wreck on gastronomic shoals.

In the United States the players were on the road 33 days. About that number of banquets were tendered. Train schedules knocked out a few. The athletes stood up manfully to the balance, even though groggy when they encountered a 125-pound cake, donated by a railroad company, at Seattle. By the time they had run the gauntlet of another score or so abroad, the party had come to the conclusion that the warmth of the greetings had nothing to do with the size of the town. The ceremonies in Blue Rapids, Kansas, were as impressive as were those in London, even though the world's metropolis had the bulge on the gold lace.

As for the game itself, the players soon discovered that all the enthusiasm was not confined to the states. They encountered as much noise in Tokyo as they had under the lee of Coogan's Bluff and the racket which greeted the tourists in Manila developed as much lung power as did the most approved concert on a busy day in the bleachers at Comiskey's Park.

Native China, alone, showed reserve. When it comes to needless exertion, be it in noise or by muscle, the follower of Confucius hires a substitute. Perhaps the fact that the only game pulled off in the Flowery Kingdom was played in "Happy Valley," on the edge of a betombed hillside from which it gets its name, had something to do with the subdued greetings from the pig-tailed spectators.

Shanghai, which figured earlier in the itinerary, undoubtedly would have made the boys feel at home had a game been possible. They had prepared for our coming for weeks and many had trained for the big event until it was hard to tell, when we arrived in a drizzle, whether they were wetter on the outside than inside. A couple of American warships were anchored in the river and it was easy to surmise that Jack Tar would not have permitted the staging of a funeral.

Australia was genuinely cordial but not exuberant. Cricket enthusiasm, the ne plus ultra in cheering, predominated despite the fact that New South Wales alone boasts of several baseball leagues. In Ceylon, Hindu and Parsee, Mohammedan and Singhalese, gathered in large numbers to gaze and marvel. At Cairo the Bedouin removed himself to a safe distance, squatted on his haunches, entrusted his soul to Allah and silently awaited the finish.

What the descendants of the Caesars thought we never had an opportunity to find out as rain blotted out the games scheduled for the Eternal City. At Nice the Gaul contributed an abundance of "vivas," but the mercurial Parisian was given no chance to berate the umpire as it never stopped raining while we were there.

Charles A. Comiskey has the distinction of being the first club-owner to use special trains to carry his players across the country. In this wintry picture, "Commy" is shown standing in the snow of Chicago just before the White Sox palace-on-wheels left on the spring training trip. Standing to the right of the Old Roman is James J. Callahan; at the left is "Big Ed" Walsh. The sign on the observation car advertises the "cargo" and its destination. These specials were renowned not only for the luxuriousness of their fittings, but also for the sumptuous assortment of food and drink provided by the Old Roman. The dispatchers ran the trains on special schedules which permitted the travelers to "visit" on the way.

XIV. Dig Spikes in Five Continents

How the English regarded the game we knew. Back in 1874, before the National League was organized, teams from Boston and Philadelphia had visited Great Britain. The cheering had been subdued and the enthusiasm was only slightly accentuated when Spalding's tourists invaded the island fifteen years later. The Prince of Wales, later Edward VII, lent social glamour to the sport in 1889. The accounts do not show that the prince was excessively demonstrative, even though interested. Twenty-five years later his son, then the king and emperor, permitted the royal smile to grow into a laugh as he watched the antics of coachers and rooters. Thirty thousand Britishers laughed with him. George applauded and the cheers of Norman and Saxon circled the field. A thaw had set in after a quarter of a century.

As has been pointed out, it had been no sudden decision on Comiskey's part to visit the farthest corners of the globe in order to have two representative baseball teams rub elbows with coolie and king. Only the plan was matured during the season of 1913. "Commy" approached McGraw on the subject. The manager of the Giants was busy winning the bunting in the National League. Comiskey had high hopes of duplicating the performance in the American. Two pennant winners were bound to make a stir and so the agreement was made. Comiskey failed to land the flag. Had he won the White Sox would have gone intact. Only seven of those making the trip wore while stockings the season following. Of these six were under Comiskey and one took orders from McGraw. James J. Callahan, manager; Jim Scott, Joe Benz, Thomas D. Daly, Andrew Slight and George Weaver made up the bona fide members. Urban Faber had signed a contract with the Sox but was turned over to the Giants for the trip. The balance of "Commy's" team was composed of Sam Crawford, Detroit Tigers; Steve Evans, St. Louis Cardinals; Tris Speaker, Boston Red Sox; Richard J. Egan, Cincinnati Nationals;

Walter F. Leverenz, St. Louis Browns; John J. A. Bliss, Pacific Coast League; Herman Schaefer, Washington Americans.

Manager McGraw picked from his own team Larry Doyle, Bunny Hearne, George R. Wiltse, Fred Merkle and James Thorpe. From outside the home circle he obtained Lee Magee and Ivy Wingo of the St. Louis Cardinals; Hans Lobert and M. J. Doolan of the Philadelphia Nationals, and Urban Faber from the White Sox. Mike Donlin, famous league star, forsook the footlights and joined McGraw's troupe.

The National Commission assigned William J. Klem from the National League and John F. Sheridan from the American as umpires. The games were played under Commission rules and the umpires had power to discipline the players as they saw fit. The arbitrators ruling with an iron hand, the playing rivalry was as bitter as during the regular season.

Tris Speaker represented the sentiment of the players in this respect when, after a tough break for the Sox in the game at Hongkong, he gave voice to this protest:

"This trip would have been a great success if we had only dropped the umpires overboard in the middle of the Pacific."

The tour began Oct. 17, when the Sox left for Cincinnati to meet the Giants in the first game, which they lost 11 to 2. After the return engagement at Chicago the Sox were not again to inhale the ozone of the Great Lakes for 142 days.

The two teams left home in the finest special train ever turned out. It consisted of six cars, a combination buffet, a diner, an observation car and three sleepers. In this hotel on wheels they lived, with stationary intervals at Los Angeles and San Francisco, until they reached Seattle. During that time they zigzagged from Chicago to central Illinois, through Iowa, Kansas, Missouri, Arkansas, Oklahoma, Texas, Arizona, California, Oregon and Washington.

Thirty-one games were played between Cincinnati and Puget Sound. Three days it rained. One game was a tie and the athletes pulled into Seattle with fifteen victories apiece. The players spent twenty-three successive nights on the sleepers. In between were wordy scraps on the field, banquets and receptions. Due to the intense rivalry one-half of the party hardly spoke to the other when the steamer Empress of Japan was boarded at Victoria, but the differences were wiped out in the common sufferings of the next seventeen days.

In the number of people played to, the money taken in and the enthusiasm displayed no trip has ever equaled this world tour. Blue Rapids, Kansas, a speck on the prairies and not much more than that in the census register, turned over $2,800 as its contribution. The town claimed a population of 1,800. At San Francisco, the fans overflowed from the stands into the field. At Medford, Oregon, the committee in charge insisted on paying $1,000, despite protests of McGraw and Callahan for the privilege of seeing teams play a few innings in pouring rain.

At Dennison, Texas, where no game was scheduled, members of the Elks' lodge with hundreds of other townspeople, stayed up until midnight in order to shanghai the athletes. At Portland, Oregon, the Chamber of Commerce staged a gilded banquet and presented a silken American flag, which was carried around the world and now has a place of honor in the Woodland Bards' room at Comiskey Park.

No one set of players could stand the strain on the trip overland and substitutions were frequent. Christy Mathewson and Chief Myers served as a battery part of the time for the Giants. Walter Johnson, the great pitcher of the Washington team, pitched for the White Sox at Tulsa, Oklahoma. The appearance of the American League speed king marked the one and only pitching duel between him and Christy Mathewson. The result was a shutout of 6 to 0 in favor of the Sox, Matty being in poor condition.

On the Sox team at different times figured Hal Chase, Doc White, Frank Isbell, Ray Schalk, Morris Rath, Lefty Russell, Walter Mattick and Joe Berger. Snodgrass, Tesreau and Fromme helped out the Giants.

The strenuous program on land and the monotonous turn of the propeller at sea required variations, as many of the players belonged to that species which hates daylight. Cards furnished the most acceptable amusement. Singing and reading made up a part. Dancing attracted many. Our national game of draw had the majority of devotees. John McGraw was captain of the whist crew, which on shipboard invariably included the commander of the vessel. Bill Klem, Fred Merkle, and Mike Donlin disturbed the serenity by their pinochle game.

In one corner of the card room on ship were found the "seven up" fiends. Jim Mullin, Tom Lynch, Joe Farrell and Billy Buhl, all Chicago business men, were the regulars. A seat was always reserved for Comiskey, who, when well enough to "sit in," always won, but never collected, as at some time or other someone always started a riot claiming "low," and this invariably broke up the game.

Comiskey's specialties were "seven up" and "hearts." He was equally keen on both. During the years he served as manager of the Cincinnati team he always spent his winters in Chicago. The gathering place for the "boys" was Mike's back room at Lytle and Twelfth streets. On one occasion the usual party, according to "Commy," had been engrossed in the game for hours before one of the players remarked on the shaky condition of the club room.

"I think Mike believes that the load he is carrying is getting too heavy and he is fixing up the foundation," suggested"Commy," as the regular battle for the possession of the two spot was on.

The jolting and groaning increased until a sudden lurch landed chairs, tables and players in a corner of the room. Getting to their feet they obtained the first glimpse of the landscape since they had sat down. The back fence had disappeared and instead there was an unobstructed vista of the street. Mike was moving to new quarters, but, as they were regular customers he didn't want to disturb them although, from force of circumstances, the service during the trip had been somewhat irregular. The game was finished on a new foundation.

Comiskey was a natural card player. Besides having that unique gift of "card sense" his marvelous memory stood him in good stead. Except in his younger days he never played poker, or any other gambling game. He never has speculated, as he always insisted in having the goods in plain view.

As the draft of both ball players and camp followers for the world tour had been selective each was expected to render some particular service, either on the ball field or in the reception room. The heavy parts were assigned to Weaver, Scott, Benz, Slight, Evans, Merkle and Schaefer as singers. Evans and Schaefer also doubled in comedy. Joe Farrell, plain tourist, was director of "stunts." Norris L. O'Neill and Harry L. Sparrow paid the bills, while Comiskey, Callahan and McGraw absorbed the kicks. After each close game Bill Klem and John F. Sheridan, as umpires, played the role of outcasts. Before each contest Klem was usually introduced as the world's greatest announcer.

To Jim Thorpe and his girl bride belonged the distinction of being the only real "native" Americans in the party, an honor reflecting glory on the tribe of Sacs and Foxes. Jap, Australian, Hindu and Roman looked admiringly on the Indian Apollo, the world's greatest individual athlete, and one of the few who, on a certain occasion, refused the invitation to chat with a king.

Others had specialties which they exhibited as occasion offered, but those mentioned made the big "noise." To the writer was assigned the task of being the Boswell to the party and to serve as foil to inquisitive foreign journalists. The events here recorded, even though incomplete, have at least the merit of being personal observations.

It was such a versatile bunch that boarded the Empress of Japan, of the Canadian Pacific Steamship line, at Victoria, B. C., on the evening of Nov. 19, after a hurried trip from Seattle on a coastwise steamer. Many were left at the dock who wanted to go. A few were missing who had been expected to accompany the party. Napoleon Lajoie, one of the greatest second basemen and batters that ever graced the game, had been originally slated to round out the Sox infield. Callahan approached him on the subject during the summer.

"Clear around the world, did you say?" queried Nap.

"Sure. And you will be back in time for the regular season," added Callahan by way of a convincing argument.

"Fine! I am with you, but I suppose it will all be by land," cautiously inquired the Cleveland star.

Callahan, knowing Lajoie's aversion to the vasty deep, explained that the bridge builders had been slow in linking up the continents, but the water trips would only be a hop, skip and jump.

"Too damp a prospect," was Lajoie's laconic rejoinder.

As the Cleveland manager would not even accompany his team on the boat between Cleveland and Detroit during the playing season his aversion to the deep might be appreciated. He must have chuckled at the narrow escape while reading how the Sox and Giants were bounced from wave to wave for seventeen consecutive days.

President Comiskey, who had started touring back in the Eighties, dodged the banquet trail across the continent, and joined the teams in San Francisco. With him was Mrs. Comiskey. Lou Comiskey and his wife made a third bridal pair in the party. Although not in the best of health Mrs. C. A. Comiskey proved to be a good sailor. As a mascot she upheld her reputation as the White Sox did better than winning the "odd" in the final reckoning.

Anticipating the constitutional amendment on sex equality and in honor of the "ladies' day," which had been inaugurated at the White Sox Ball Park, nearly as many women as men were included in the strictly tourist party. Of the "baseball wives" there were Mrs. C. A. Comiskey, Mrs. Lou Comiskey, Mrs. J. J. Callahan and her mother, Mrs. D. Hardin, Mrs. John McGraw, Mrs. James Thorpe, Mrs. H. Lobert, Mrs. Samuel Crawford, Mrs. L. Doyle, Mrs. George Wiltse and Mrs. W. J. Klem.

The rest of the roll call included Mrs. H. E. Keough, Miss Margaret Callahan, Mrs. N. S. McLean, Mr. and Mrs. James R. McAleer, Mr. and Mrs. James J. Mullin, Mr. and Mrs. Joseph C. Farrell, Mr. and Mrs. William C. Buhl, N. E. McBride, Master Daniel Callahan, Ted Sullivan, A. P. Anderson, Norris L. O'Neill, Thomas E. Lynch, William Ryan, Frank T. Farrell, Harry L. Sparrow, G. W. Axelson, James Hill, Albert Kenney, Frank McGlynn, Victor Miller, Dr. Frank Finley and Father McNamara.

After the strenuous transcontinental trip the majority of the tourists were ready for a night's rest after having boarded the "Empress." The berths furnished the opportunity, but that was all. Within twelve hours Father Neptune had laid low four-fifths of the party. Joe Farrell went along to furnish cheer and anecdotes to the travelers. On the third day he dragged himself to the wireless and sent to Chicago this message: "All well except the passengers." He did not exaggerate.

On the seventh day out I lost touch with land, the last wireless message sent my newspaper in Chicago having been forwarded from a distance of 1,800 miles. Then for almost eight days we were "lost." Few cared, as it was blowing between "11 and 12" most of the time.

In copying the log from Captain Dixon-Hopcroft's records I innocently inquired what would have happened had it blown "No. 13." The man who slept neither night or day, trying to keep the ship afloat, wearily glanced in my direction, but that was all.

I related the incident to the first mate. He also assumed a pained look but consented to explain to a land lubber that 12 was the last number in reckoning the velocity of wind, calm being zero.

Such unseemly behavior on the part of a "peaceful ocean," although it floored most of the athletes, did not entirely blot out the social functions in the smoking room. While the tableware in the dining saloon was "racked" and the chairs lassoed, there were always enough on hand to enjoy the scenery and shuffle the cards.

Herman Schaefer, who shared with Nick Altrock, up to the time he died last year, the honor of comedian in chief of the ball field, was a steady contributor to the game of draw. "The Dutchman," as he was best known to his friends, had many peculiarities on and off the playing field. In the indoor game he developed a violent antipathy against anyone who stayed on "shorts." It happened that Herman, who opened the pot with a pair of aces and finished with "ups" was beaten by Umpire Sheridan, who had drawn three cards to a pair of fives. Schaefer tossed the deck out of the window and left the table in high dudgeon, vowing that he never would make good his end of the pot, which amounted to $6. The card room saw him no more that day, but he dropped in on the boys the following morning. Dumping a hat full of coppers in front of Sheridan he remarked: "Here's what I owe you."

The collection included everything in base metal that went for currency the world around, and it amounted to just $6, based on international exchange as expressed in weight. Schaefer had spent the better part of the day in collecting the junk from white, black, Chink and Malay, and it cost him twice as much as he originally owed Sheridan.

There was considerable rivalry between Evans and Schaefer. Steve was a born imitator and a wit of the first order. Returning to New York after the trip he described to Jim Gilmore and John B. Ward of the Federal League how he felt when he first wore a silk hat on the trip. The story made such a hit that the Brooklyn owner signed him for twice as much as he could get from the National League. On the ship from Freemantle to Suez he masqueraded as an Englishman and got away with it. In order to catch up Schaefer, on his arrival at Nice, signed himself on the hotel register as "Prince Henry." Every bellboy in the place was at his beck and call, much to the discomfiture of the rest of the guests.

Larry Doyle, one of the bridegrooms of the party, was the chief practical joker. Larry was responsible for the story of the two sets of "fours." He detailed it around the world and dwelt pathetically on the tragedy of the possessor of two pairs of threes, who swallowed a six-inch perfecto, ashes and all, when, after a long siege, he was given the privilege of gazing on four fives in the hands of John Sheridan. The possessor of the losing hand denies the yarn, as he did not smoke during that particular period of the journey.

Occasionally the staid members of the party joined in the fun. James Mullin and Thomas Lynch, substantial men of business, figured in one episode. With most everybody being "in" on it except Ted Sullivan, the man who brought out Comiskey, a game with loaded dice was arranged between Mullin and Lynch. When the game was over Lynch was "strapped." Ted was told about it and went to "Commy." The latter knew nothing about it, but scented a "frame-up," and told Sullivan that the Captain should be informed.

The skipper listened to the sad tale and ordered Mullin to the brig. Comiskey refused to interfere and it took all of Sullivan's persuasive powers to get the captain to relent.

Umpire Klem was another victim. Just out of Manila there had

"Commy"

With the departure of the White Sox and Giants on the world tour, the well-wishes of the country went with them. Cartoonist Briggs has caught the spirit of leave-taking—Uncle Sam at the end of the pier gazing sort o' lonesome-like at the fading ship which was to carry the tourists on the longest trip ever taken by a ball team.

been much conversation on what would happen when the ship should cross the "line." Steve Evans publicly announced an interview with the captain to the effect that the speed of the ship would be increased as soon as it had gone over the top at the equator as it would be downhill the rest of the way unless the vessel should be snagged by the "line" on the equator.

At the appointed time Steve rushed into the smoking room and proclaimed that the ship had practically stopped as it had been unable to hurdle the line, which was now dragging on both sides. Everybody rushed to the side of the vessel. Evans insisted that Klem hung over the rail for two hours looking for the equatorial tow.

Klem evened up on the way north. At the coming on board of King Neptune, arrayed in all his royal finery of sea weeds and burlap, some of the umpire's tormentors got the ducking of their lives, much to the amusement of Miss Margaret Callahan and Master Daniel Callahan, children of the manager of the Sox and official mascots.

Comiskey himself could not always join in the festivities, as acute stomach troubles [not sea sickness] robbed him of much of the pleasure on the trip. He showed gameness to the core, however, by seldom missing a reception on land when etiquette demanded his presence. He refused to be floored until a world famous specialist at Rome ordered him to bed. Whether, when he arrived off Sandy Hook, he had the stormy days of the Pacific in mind or the heroic doses of bismuth administered at Rome, was not clear, but it must have been one or the other, as each furnished an impelling argument against leaving home.

Here and there a light could be discerned in the distance through the snowy haze when John McGraw sought out Comiskey.

"I want you to get up early in the morning," suggested McGraw. "I'd like to have you see the Statue of Liberty."

"Think I will, John," answered the "Old Roman," "for if she looks me in the face again she will have to turn around."

◆ CHAPTER XV ◆

Baseball Thrills for a King

Governor General of Australia taught a new "curve"—Sir Thomas Lipton and Schaefer are chummy—Pilgrims meet the Pope—Find a baseball fan in the Vatican—Nine balls and three strikeouts—A rookie wins an eleven inning thriller before a king—A new toast.

The tour headed by "Commy" offered a lesson in preparedness. It was like traveling by megaphone on a rubber-neck wagon. All knew where they were going and what was expected of them when they got there. Social usages could thus be adhered to and the members would leave the impression that they had been born equally to the purple and the homespun.

If conviviality was on the cards, good fellowship would be on tap without stint; if dignity better comported to the surroundings, no one was apprehensive of "breaks." Each member had been trained to his individual dress suit and top hat. Occasionally a brain storm produced variety.

Nearing Japan one of the athletes came into the dining room, direct from the sick ward, arrayed in a swallow tail coat with all the trimmings down to the patent leather pumps but with white stockings, embroidered on the instep with a flaming monogram in blue.

On another occasion, in crossing the Mediterranean, a pilgrim threw the German head steward into spasms by appearing in "evening" dress consisting of a claw-hammer coat, black vest, negligee shirt, four-in-hand red necktie, white trousers and slippers.

"Why did you do it?" asked an embarrassed fellow traveler.

"To prove that it could be done," was the noncommittal answer.

As a matter of fact back of it was a conspiracy to make the custom of the English, in dressing for dinner, look ridiculous. Adjusting shirt studs took too much time away from the game.

On land it behooved the visitors to be on their guard when out of their baseball uniforms, as there was hardly a mile covered where they were not officially chaperoned. Arriving at quarantine at Yokohama the party was met by the personal representatives of the mayor and the Japanese and American governments. They were considered guests of the nation until they departed from Nagasaki.

At Hongkong not only did the English governor turn over "Happy Valley," which was government property and incidentally the only level piece of ground on the island, for the game, but the port authorities permitted the tourists to leave the Empress of Japan and board the St. Albans, after the former had sailed into the harbor with the yellow flag at its mast head. At Manila Governor Harrison and Generals Franklin J. Bell and H. P. McCain saw to it that nothing was left undone for the visitors' comfort.

Beginning at Thursday Island, the northernmost landing place in Australia for ships taking the route inside the great Barrier Reef, official and private hospitality never missed a cog. At every stop, city, state and commonwealth dignitaries vied with each other in making the stay pleasant. As games were played in the afternoons, receptions were confined to mornings while banquets held sway in the evenings, usually followed by theatre parties. The fact that champagne and cakes were served at the official receptions in the city halls at Sydney and Melbourne immediately after the "ham and" made a considerable impression.

Speeches were the order everywhere. For the tourists several members were adept at the act. The heavy work devolved on Callahan, McGraw and Ted Sullivan. As Callahan, in "Gentleman Jim," had capitalized his story telling ability on the stage and as Sullivan had followed the profession of lecturer, many a host was given the impression that we carried professional speech-makers with us. McGraw was equally at home on the platform and the party scored a perfect average in this line. Comiskey, who had an aversion to appearing in public, did not always escape. What he had to say was usually taken down stenographically.

In Melbourne Lord Denham, the governor general and all-around good sportsman, entertained the entire party, assisted by Lady Denham. Then to show how Great Britain's representative in the antipodes appreciated the visit he pitched the first ball in the initial contest on the Melbourne Cricket Club's grounds. He became enthusiastic and inquisitive about the game and insisted on learning all about the mysteries of pitching, he himself being a star cricket player.

At Colombo, Ceylon, Sir Thomas J. Lipton anticipated all others by sending a radio message as soon as contact could be had with the steamship Orontes, asking the party to be his guests while on the island. He proved a capital host and an unaffected and democratic good fellow.

Passing through the dining room of the Sox-Giants' hotel at dinner, the millionaire sportsman espied Herman Schaefer, with others, at a table.

"Is everything all right," queried Sir Thomas.

"Tom, I never enjoyed myself more in my life," ejaculated the "prince," to the horror of highborn Britons in the room.

"Herman, you are on for an automobile ride after dinner, you know," was the ready response of the knighted tea merchant, and everybody laughed.

Sir Thomas stuck to the finish. He went out with the final boat load at midnight and the last glimpse his guests had of the jolly Irishman they saw him standing in a rowboat waving his hat and trying to compete with the hoarse toots of the siren as the Orontes picked its way out of the harbor.

Not much had been expected in Egypt and it occasioned surprise when the khedive, Abbas Hilmi II, appeared at the first game, played on the grounds at Heliopolis. Abbas Hilmi laid aside his royal reserve for the time being and talked baseball. That someone had posted him in advance was evident. Before he left, which was in the seventh inning, he thanked Comiskey for his visit and hoped that he could "come again." If such should be the case Abbas probably would not be among those present. A few months later he fell on evil ways and picked the wrong side in the great war.

Lord Kitchener, the Earl of Khartoum, who was virtual viceroy of Egypt, was expected to see the Sox and Giants in action, but at the last minute, was compelled to send his regrets.

Many of the tourists being of the Catholic faith it was but natural that the papal reception at Rome should make a deep impression. The meeting with Pope Pius IX was simplicity itself. After a talk by Msgr. Kennedy of the American College at Rome, the pilgrims were introduced and their mission explained. The Holy Father listened intently and the ceremony was concluded by the blessing of the visitors.

The democratic ways of the papal secretary, Cardinal Merry del Val, made a hit with everybody. Here in the Vatican itself the members of the party found a high dignitary of the church able to converse with them not only in their own tongue, but in the language of the diamond as well. As proof of his intimate knowledge of the game was a picture hanging on the wall in the cardinal's apartments, showing him in baseball uniform.

"Yes, I thought I could play the game pretty well once," said the cardinal. "I considered myself useful in the infield on the college team at Baltimore, and I suppose the manager agreed for he kept me in the lineup quite a while."

Prior to the visit to Rome Comiskey had been presented with a bronze statue of the Discus Thrower, in Naples. This followed after a delegation of sporting clubs had met the party at the docks. The presentation speech was made by Hall Caine, the English novelist, who was in Naples at the time. On landing the party had been met by Dr. John Edward Jones, United States consul general at Genoa, who stayed with the bunch until the French border was reached.

At Nice the players added to the gaiety of the world-famous carnival, which was at its height when they arrived. They were given a prominent place in the parade and were almost buried under a shower of confetti.

Although no game could be played in Paris the social conquest continued, a reception by Ambassador Myron T. Herrick featuring the entertainment. A banquet was tendered by Julius Kessler, an American citizen residing in Paris.

In London reception followed reception, the official luncheon at the Savoy Hotel rounding out the day and night entertainments. At this ornate affair official circles were represented by Lord Desborough and Lord Lonsdale while Consul General Griffith responded for the United States.

Although personal gratification played a part in the world tour, Comiskey insisted from the beginning that the game would have to be the thing. The trip, in his estimation, should accomplish two objects. In addition to introducing our national sport into foreign lands the members would also carry a message of international concord. In this respect, were he inclined to stretch a point, President Comiskey might look back with pardonable pride to the coincidence that, of the ten political entities visited, all were found on the side of the Allies when the great test came.

Of advantage to the travelers, as well as lending prestige to their comings and goings, was the aid extended by the Washington administration. At the direction of President Wilson, Secretary of State William Jennings Bryan had, weeks in advance, notified diplomatic and consular offices in every city to be visited, to extend all the help and courtesies possible.

Instructions of the promoters, issued at the start, included a fiat against hippodroming on the ball field. This was faithfully followed out but the Keio University baseball team came to the conclusion in the first international clash that the dictum was not observed. The Sox had whipped the Giants in the initial set-to on foreign soil before as big a mob as had ever seen a game in Tokyo. Then it came the turn of the university team, the best in Nippon, to defend the honors of the Mikado's realm.

Jim Scott, the man with the "round-house" curve, was given the job of pitching for the amalgamated team against the Japs. Scott had been one of the sickest of the sick on the trans–Pacific trip and it took several innings before he could find his land legs. Consequently after a strikeout Center Fielder Morri smote him for a triple and Nyaka's single made run No. 1 for Keio. Getting the first tally in the game against what was regarded as the champion combination of the universe so worked on the nerves of the rooters that a madhouse would have furnished the scenario for a lullaby in comparison. The fact that the one run lead was wiped out in the Sox half made no difference. They had scored on a team which had come 7,000 miles to show them how to play the game.

Eventually the Japs accumulated two more runs while the Sox-Giants ran up sixteen. That was deemed a fair ratio but the sting came in the final inning, with Keio at bat. Scott, having settled down, was in his best form and, pitching just nine balls, struck out the side. Nothing could be plainer than that the visitors had been hippodroming in the other eight rounds. Explanations having been made the entente cordiale was restored. The short stay was triumphantly brought to a close when Fred Merkle, in the third and final game, put the ball over the left field fence, a feat that had been deemed impossible by every follower of the game in Tokyo.

It was also in that farewell performance that the natives saw a play which McGraw insisted was the greatest he himself had ever seen. It was a peg from deep center field which caught Mike Donlin coming in from third. Lobert had hit a regular skyscraper, and Tris Speaker, who had started to sprint with the crack of the bat, picked the ball off a Nipponese top-knot in the bleachers. Whirling without being set for the throw he shot the ball to Jack Bliss at the plate, who nailed the oncoming Mike by a step. The out came near ruining the trip for Donlin, who called on all the saints in the calendar to bear witness to the fact that the ball which killed him off was not the one which Lobert had hit.

Before every contest a "shadow game," in which the players went through the motions without the aid of a ball, was staged. This made a big hit all the way from Chicago to London. The Japs saw it before the first game and became adept at it before the second had been played. It was the same with the Filipinos, but to the matter-of-fact subjects of King George it proved a puzzle to the end. At Brisbane two Englishmen stood watching the antics of the players. Both became deeply engrossed.

"What celerity," remarked one.

"Righto," interjected the other one. "I cawn't even see the ball, you know."

The Japanese, true to their natural bent, insisted on getting the hang of every trick. The Filipinos proved as adaptive. Herman Schaefer had the knack of throwing the ball behind his back in any direction he desired. He gave an exhibition of his skill at Manila. The following forenoon the ball was similarly juggled on every lot in the city and there were plenty of prairie diamonds as, according to the chief of police, 200 games were played each Sunday.

Although there are some good Chinese ball teams in various parts of the world the natives stood in stolid silence and watched the performance in "Happy Valley," Hongkong. The yells were furnished by thousands of sailors, representing practically every navy on earth. In the forefront were American jackies, who had not seen a game for a year.

Intermittent battles with the elements marked the tour. The teams were wafted out of Shanghai on a midwinter monsoon. The second game in Manila was played on a field that had been six inches under water twenty minutes before the game started. Drought prevailed in Australia. In Rome and Paris the downpour never let up and it was not dusty in London.

The playing fields proved much better than had been expected. The cricket fields in Queensland, New South Wales and Victoria furnished carpeted playing surfaces. Other diamonds were mostly of the "skinned" variety. On all, the brand of ball was up to the standard. One of the marvelous exhibitions was the last contest at Manila, where an errorless seven-inning game had been played on a field which resembled a morass.

The first native team in Australia was encountered at Sydney. It "borrowed" Wiltse and Wingo as a battery but lost 10 to 1 in a five-inning game. In a seven-inning contest the following day a team composed entirely of home talent went down to a 15 to 2 defeat. The score of 18 to 0 in favor of the Giants decorated the board at Melbourne.

At Sydney the "Old Roman" tried his hand at cricket. An expert handed up the ball.

"I should think I ought to be able to knock the ball out of the lot with a paddle like that," remarked "Commy" as he took his place in front of the wicket.

He did not "lose" the ball but retired with the laurels of having protected his wicket.

A game had been scheduled at Freemantle, West Australia, but on arrival the tourists discovered that the local committee had forgotten to make arrangements for a playing field. A sight-seeing trip to Perth was taken instead, a place where Comiskey enjoyed the distinction of going broke. He had his letter of credit for $121,000 and a $20 gold piece when he arrived. When he tried to settle for dinner he proffered the double eagle. Nothing like it had ever been seen. He tried the bank. Being experts on the yellow metal in this part of the world, which produces a fair share of it, it was pronounced gold but not currency. The bank finally took a chance but nicked him $1.40 for the trouble.

Leaving the lone continent behind on Jan. 14 the next exhibition contest was put on at Colombo a week later, without price but with a lot of ceremony. The race track inclosure was used for playing field. The ground was rough and it rained part of the time. Sir Thomas Lipton and the American consul said they enjoyed it. The natives were non-committal.

It was a lazy journey from the land of tea and cinnamon into the Red sea, which despite its name didn't appear red after all to some of our tourists.

XV. Baseball Thrills for a King

After having had a distant glimpse of the town of Aden, the fourth continent in the itinerary, brown and treeless, burst upon the view during the latter part of January.

The prospect of playing before the Sphinx impressed the globe trotters more than did the privilege of pulling off a game before the khedive. The morning after the pilgrims had landed at Suez they stood before the mutilated but majestic figure of the desert enigma.

"Whoever said we could stage a game here must have been in league with the picture card trust," said Comiskey as he surveyed the 30 by 40 playing field in front of the inscrutable one.

"That's one of Stoney Face's riddles," suggested the scholarly Egan.

"Kidding us, I should say," added McGraw as the moving picture brigade adjusted their tripods.

"Well, let us go through the motions and kid posterity," suggested Callahan, and through the motions they went to the accompaniments of clicking cameras and shouting donkey drivers. That was as much of a game as has ever been staged before the Sphinx.

Athletes and camp followers, having listened to the ravings of Arab sheiks, explored the pyramid of Giza to its innermost depths and regretted the venture.

Bruised and weary the gazers on Egyptian antiquities moved to the other side of the Nile six miles beyond Cairo for two real ball games. The first one went to a 3 to 3 tie in ten innings. It again gave the lie to hippodroming as it was marked by much confusion of tongues, the exposing of family skeletons and a general truculency on part of the players, each side now trying to get the edge on games won.

A few white folks having missed the first contest a second was staged the following day. The Giants won 6 to 3 and pulled off a triple play, the only one on the trip. Both games were played on the

Heliopolis grounds, a level expanse of desert, the boundaries being marked by rows of stately palms with a background of botanical gardens, a handsome clubhouse and attractive villas.

Only two games followed the two days' journey across the Mediterranean, which was made on the German steamer Prinz Heinrich. The short trip was marked by the absence of Umpire Sheridan and the appearance of a pilsner brew. Sheridan had missed the boat in the confusion of embarkation at Alexandria and did not catch up with the party until London was reached. Those of Teuton extraction found some consolation in the amber fluid.

With the game at Nice on Feb. 16, 1914, the Sox and Giants had dug their spikes into five continents. The lead remained with the former, as Comiskey's crew won the game 10 to 9. With the carnival program over and the drizzle of Paris only a memory London alone remained on the schedule.

After jockeying with uncertain weather conditions it was finally decided to play February 26. The Chelsea Football Field, within the Stamford Bridge grounds, which had been dedicated to the game by Spalding's pioneers, was selected as being the most suitable. Then loyal American enthusiasts, led by John Lambert, George Grant, now owner of the Boston Nationals, and others, started to get court circles interested. They had just twenty-four hours to do it in. As soon as apprised of the game the king assured ambassador Page that he would be on hand. He was there at the appointed time with thirty thousand other Britons.

As it happened his majesty saw the greatest thriller of the entire trip. Spectacular catches followed prodigious swats, a home-run drive by Tom Daly winding up the sensational contest in the eleventh inning. It is a question as to what impressed the king the more, the riotous rooting of the Americans or the circus feats of the players. For the former he made use of Ambassador Page as interpreter. He

Snapped on the world tour—Urban Faber (left) who pitched an 11-inning contest before King George of England; Tom Daly (right) whose home-run swat won the game for the White Sox.

could make notes of the stunts without any special help. The one-hand catch by Magee of Speaker's terrific drive over the running track in left field needed no explanation. It was unnecessary to expound the beauties of Daly's eleventh inning drive or to explain that it was the longest hit ever made within the historic grounds.

The mighty wallop spelled finis for a remarkable baseball trip. It had been successful from every angle and Comiskey had the satisfaction of having piloted a team to victory during the trip that was now in possession of the globe circling baseball title. "Commy's" team accumulated a total of 24 wins; McGraw's crowd drew 20.

Fifty games had been played in all, those with native teams making up the difference.

The winning hit in that closing contest was made off Urban Faber, who had been loaned to the Giants for the trip. No rookie had been put to a more severe test than was the youngster from Cascade, Iowa. Not only was it up to him to hold his own against Jim Scott and Joe Benz, veteran slabsmen, but in addition, he was pitching under the gaze of a monarch and a great crowd of diplomatic notables.

Faber blamed himself for the defeat of his team but McGraw did not. When next the Giants and the Sox met, three and a half years later, it was Faber again who held the spotlight. By winning three out of six games from the Giants for the White Sox, he added another world's trophy to Comiskey's collection.

No game was ever more hard-fought than the extra-inning tempest at London. Few had been as sensational. Seldom had the spectators been as numerous. The White Sox scored first—two runs in the third inning on singles by Evans, Bliss and Weaver, and a base on balls to Scott. Lobert's home-run to center, back of an error by Schaefer on Magee's grounder, made it a tie in the fourth. For the Giants, first to bat in the tenth, singles by Donlin and Magee, a sacrifice hit by Lobert and a fielder's choice and an out, brought two runs.

It appeared as if Broadway would have the opportunity to celebrate, but Weaver, in the Sox half, started to even it up with a single. Egan went out on an infield tap. Speaker's drive had the earmarks of a home-run but Magee, sprinting as he had never done before, made a leap in the air and speared the ball with one hand. Disgusted, Speaker yelled:

"Yes, you lucky stiff. You tried that grand stand play eleven times on the trip without making it and now you pulled it off before a king."

Sam Crawford caused the second tie of the game by sending the ball a trifle higher than had Tris. There was no need to reach for this. It never was found.

The Giants were blanked in their half of the eleventh. Daly was the first up for the Sox. It was rookie against rookie and royalty looked on both. Faber tried to squeeze one by on the inside. He made a poor guess. Where the ball went no one cared. Donlin, in center field, took one look at and made a break for the shower. King and commoner arose, stretched and agreed that they had seen "some game." His Majesty told Ambassador Page that he had never enjoyed an afternoon more. This he repeated to Comiskey and McGraw through his chamberlain, who conveyed the appreciation of the king to the leaders of the tour at their hotel. Previously he had shaken hands with both in the royal box where he held a democratic pow-wow before the game.

The scorer did not wish to entrust the box score to cricket-playing cable operators so the complete statistics of the game are now given for the first time:

White Sox	AB	R	H	TB	BB	SH	SB	P	A	E
Weaver, ss	5	1	3	3	0	0	0	3	3	0
Egan, 3b	3	0	0	0	1	1	0	0	3	0
Speaker, cf	5	0	0	0	0	0	0	2	0	0
Crawford, rf	5	1	2	5	0	0	0	1	0	0
Schaefer, 2b	4	0	0	0	0	0	0	1	2	1
Daly, 1b	5	1	1	4	0	0	0	17	0	0
Evans, lf	4	1	2	2	0	0	0	3	0	0
Bliss, c	2	1	1	1	0	0	0	2	1	0
Scott, p	1	0	0	0	1	0	0	0	2	0
Slight, c	2	0	2	2	0	0	0	4	1	0
Benz, p	2	0	0	0	0	0	0	0	5	0
Total	38	5	11	17	2	1	0	33	17	1

Giants	AB	R	H	TB	BB	SH	SB	P	A	E
Donlin, cf	5	1	2	3	0	0	0	2	1	0

GIANTS	AB	R	H	TB	BB	SH	SB	P	A	E
Magee, lf	3	2	1	1	1	0	0	4	0	0
Lobert, 3b	4	1	1	4	0	1	0	1	5	0
Doyle, 2b	4	0	1	1	1	0	0	1	6	0
Merkle, 1b	4	0	1	1	0	1	0	14	1	1
Doolan, ss	4	0	1	1	0	1	0	3	4	0
Thorpe, rf	5	0	0	0	0	0	0	1	0	0
Wingo, c	4	0	1	1	1	0	0	3	1	0
Faber, p	5	0	0	0	0	0	0	0	1	0
Total	38	4	8	12	3	3	0	*29	19	1

*Evans hit by own batted ball in 5th; none out when winning run was scored.

Score by innings:

	1	2	3	4	5	6	7	8	9	10	11
White Sox	0	0	2	0	0	0	0	0	0	2	1—5
Giants	0	0	0	2	0	0	0	0	0	2	0—4

Two base hit—Donlin. Home runs—Crawford, Daly, Lobert. Left on bases—Chicago, 7; New York, 8. Hits—Off Scott, 3 in 5 innings; off Benz, 5 in 6 innings. Struck out—By Scott, 2; by Benz, 4; by Faber, 1. Bases on balls—Off Scott, 1; off Benz, 2; off Faber, 2. Hit by pitcher—Magee by Scott; Schaefer by Faber. Wild pitch—Scott. Double plays—Lobert to Doyle to Merkle; Doyle to Doolan to Merkel. Time of game—1:50. Attendance, 35,000. Umpires—William Klem and John F. Sheridan.

As the historic tour started so did it finish—in a riot of banquets. The Lusitania was warped to its dock the morning of March 6. The evening of March 7, eight hundred fans, including many notables, crowded into the banquet hall of the new Biltmore Hotel to do honor to the returning wanderers. The White Sox fans came to New York in a special train. On arrival they chartered a steamer for their own use, stayed up all night and met the ocean liner at dawn.

Spurning sleep this heroic band of rooters, representative of every section in the middle west, took the Sox in tow on March 8, made a record run to Chicago, where they arrived the morning of the 9th, and went into training for the finishing touches of the tour.

The Congress Hotel housed the last "party," where a thousand fans rose as one to the toast:

"The White Sox! May they always win; but win or lose, the White Sox!"

◆ CHAPTER XVI ◆

Blazing New Trails

Comiskey starts roaming early—Special trains become an institution—First to train on foreign soil—Annual fall hegiras to the northern woods begin—Tale of the "blanks" and the stationary bird—An Indian uprising near Springstead—Muskie and the tenderfoot.

Roaming always had a special attraction to Comiskey. It was this trait of his character which sent him around the world. Perhaps he acquired it looking for ball fields on the prairies around Chicago when the city was young. Pioneering became a habit with him and it was a dull year when he did not discover a virgin training camp or two or lay out a new route for an exhibition tour.

The Browns afforded him his first opportunity to see the country. After having won the world's championship in 1886 he took the team to California. On the way out he played games with local teams. On the coast he met Anson's White Stockings and the Philadelphia Nationals. He repeated the western trip in 1889, playing the New York Giants and other teams.

His years in Cincinnati and the minor leagues kept him off the road until he finally settled in Chicago. In the beginning he adjusted his journeys to prospective receipts. He has yet to make a losing spring trip or exhibition jaunt. About ten years ago the Sox trained in Texas, coming north by easy stages. Another major league team, equally well advertised, covered practically the same territory. Comiskey was $6,000 ahead at the finish. The other combination lost $3,500.

Practically every team that has invaded California lost money on the venture. Comiskey took his White Sox to the Golden State in 1908 for his first far west training trip. Everybody predicted that it would cost him a lot of money.

"If it does," said Comiskey, "we will have a lot of fun spending it as we are going out in a train of our own."

It was the first special that ever rolled into a training camp. Thereafter the Sox always traveled to the spring camps by special train until the war put a stop to the luxury. Incidentally the first California tour netted the Old Roman $7,000. The train cost him an equal sum. He took similar chances in 1909, 1910, 1913, 1914 and 1915.

"How do you do it?" asked a fellow owner.

"It is all in knowing when to let go," was the answer.

Perhaps that was not the real reason, but the fact remains that Comiskey has visited more corners of the earth than any other magnate in the game. Outside of the world tour his most ambitious project was the spring training trip to the City of Mexico in 1907. He had gone to Marlin, Texas, in 1904, a journey of over 1,600 miles, and experts of the game predicted that it would be a "bloomer." As for Mexico, aside from the expenses and distance, the altitude—over 7,000 feet—would be the finish of the Sox, it was argued.

"Oh, never mind," parried the Old Roman. "Altitude won't bother the Sox. They were above everybody else in baseball last year so they are used to it."

The experiment proved a success artistically even if not financially, although the Mexicans took readily to the game. Vice-President Raymon Corall, less apt to be made a target by disappointed patriots than Porfirio Diaz, set the pace for social and political amenities. The rest of the official family fell in line and in Mexico the grand stand became a center of society.

As vociferous and insistent rooters the Mexicans run a close second to the Japs. They will become even more personal in criticism than the Nipponese if the pitcher wobbles or the batter strikes out. Big Ed Walsh, perspiring and red-necked, labored hard to get a break to the ball in the rarified atmosphere. When "otro toro" swelled to a chorus in the bleachers he interpreted it as an encouragement to his efforts until a resident American sent word to Manager Jones that the native rooters insisted on a change in pitchers. They had voiced their demands for "another bull" in no mistaken accents and ever afterwards "otro toro" had an ominous sound to the Big Moose.

Leaving the valley of the Aztecs the players were of the opinion that the two weeks under the "high sky" had been wasted. The pitchers had been unable to get a decent curve over the plate. The ball refused to "break" to the usual twist of the wrist and as for the fielders, they were helpless.

Judging a ball in that atmosphere was mere guess work. Fielder Jones, one of the greatest outfielders in the business, missed the first high fly sent in his direction by fifty feet. Frank Isbell stood under a pop-up at third base and saw it drop ten feet away from him.

"The ball weighs a ton when it comes down," complained Izzy after the game in the hearing of Comiskey.

"Well, the one I saw come down at third base didn't make your fingers sore," cut in the "Old Roman."

But training on the roof of the continent had an unexpected sequel. On the return north, playing at sea level, the pitchers discovered that they could get a better break on the ball than they ever had before. To the batters the "pill" looked like a pumpkin and had the reaction lasted the Sox probably would have broken up the league race with their sticks instead of subsiding into "hitless wonders." The explanation was that extra efforts of the pitchers and the keenness of the batters in trying to locate the ball in the Mexican altitudes contributed to increased efficiency when once they were back in natural surroundings.

In 1911 the Sox put Mineral Wells, Texas, on the map. They have trained there ever since, with the exception of two years.

For the season of 1917 Comiskey had picked the Isthmus of Panama as training grounds for his team. Lack of transportation, due to the war, put a stop to that. A South American tour still is on the program. "Commy" has expressed a wish to play at Capetown and Johannesburg. The latter place offered him $5,000 if he would include the African mining center in his world tour itinerary.

Wherever the Sox go, a trainload of camp followers are certain to be on the trail. Many found it inconvenient to go in the spring. For these "Commy" instituted the annual fall hegiras to the northern woods. Prominent men in all walks of life and from different sections of the country have been guests of Comiskey at Springstead and Mercer, Wisconsin. The Jerome Hunting and Fishing Club on Trude Lake, has achieved a national distinction.

The parties seldom have been below sixty in number. Some have been bigger. All have been lively. What the best hotels could offer in food and drink could be had at these Indian Summer camps. In addition the natives, white and red, have insisted on contributing everything that forest and stream produced.

Springstead was in the real forest primeval. The noise never disturbed the neighbors. At first there was only one—a trapper three miles away. The distance to Fifield, the nearest railroad station, was thirty-five miles. It took a day to make the trip by wagon—autos were unknown in Wisconsin woods in the days of 1903. A week was required to haul out the provisions and the party each fall was usually big enough to press into service every spare vehicle of the lumber town.

Sham battles with Indians, salutes and a craving for noise generally, required an extensive arsenal. An opportunity was offered those who boasted of their marksmanship. Ban Johnson was considered a crack shot. Spotting a bird along the roadside going in, Ban was given the try, but it was with some amazement that the travelers watched the grouse take wing after the report of the gun. Another was located and this also joined its mate. Others did likewise.

At the next halting place Johnson, without saying a word, stuck a piece of paper on a tree and blazed away at a distance of fifty feet. He apparently had made a miss with both barrels and there was a laugh all around.

Further on the guide discovered a grouse some distance in front of the first vehicle. Tom Loftus, who held the record as practical joker of the American League, was given the benefit of the first look.

"Well, here is where I show up Ban," he said, as the report reverberated through the woods.

The bird never moved.

"Give it the other barrel, Tom," encouraged Johnson, who had rushed up. The second load of No. 7 made no more impression than the first and Loftus made a motion as if to club the bird into submission. On second thought he decided to sneak up on it. Grabbing it in both hands he found it rooted to the spot, supported by stilts and tied with strings.

"Well, anyway, Ban, I got you on the blanks," said Loftus as he disengaged the very dead bird.

Springstead was only six miles from the Flambeau Chippewa

Indian reservation. One year every able-bodied member of the tribe had been engaged to give August Herrmann and other prominent politicians from Cincinnati a fitting welcome. It was to take place at night and besides the "reception," the program included a scare and a war dance. The chairman of the National Commission couldn't come, but the red fire had to be put to some use and the ammunition expended.

As luck would have it, there were several tenderfeet along who stood in need of a woodland initiation. Thus it happened that while a score or more were wrestling with busted flushes, high and low, and melded aces in the main cabin one night, a guide rushed in and announced that the Indians were coming. The lights went out in a twinkling while defensive plans were discussed in subdued tones in the darkness. Through the windows could be seen a distant shack already enveloped in a carmine fire while shots and yells rent the air.

"The cabin will be ablaze in a few minutes and we will burn like rats," suggested somebody from behind the stove.

"Only thing left is to rush 'em," proposed Comiskey.

"Don't let them get me, Commy," piped a voice from under the bed in the farthest corner of the room.

"I'll die with you, Jack," encouraged the "Old Roman" as he threw himself on top of the bed, almost knocking the wind out of the victim beneath.

Had not someone laughed as a valiant "loophound" from Chicago hit his head on the wood box trying to make a "stage" fall, some of the city bred folks might have died of fright.

The refugee under the bed got even the following day.

While he was out in a boat with Tom Loftus an eighteen pound muskie was snagged by the Dubuque magnate. The excitement of the night before had so unnerved Jack that he was in no condition to gaze with serenity on the fish as the latter almost jarred the slats loose from the side of the boat. Grabbing a revolver from the kit he emptied the contents in the general direction of the muskie's head, blew a hole in the bottom of the boat and almost drowned both.

Most of the tricks "Commy's" guests played on each other were less risky but more pointed. Courts-martial were a favorite form of amusement. These were conducted according to Hoyle, as there were always enough bona fide judges and lawyers in the party to assure even-handed justice. Some of the greatest speeches it has been my privilege to listen to I have heard in the "shack" that the Woodland Bards sing about, and all because someone had failed to "follow suite," had eaten between meals, had snored or missed roll call at tea time.

The possibilities of land and water having been exhausted at Springstead, Comiskey and his friends obtained control of the Jerome Hunting and Fishing Club, twelve miles from Mercer, in 1907. Here the Woodland Bards organized, the qualification for membership consisting in at least one visit to the camp. For eleven years the club has been open summer and winter for the friends of the White Sox owner. The two weeks immediately following the close of each baseball season made the special event.

At the last "roundup" the place consisted of 600 acres of land, all enclosed with a sixteen foot woven wire fence. Being an ardent lover of animals Comiskey started an out-door zoo, which at present consists of nearly 300 head of deer, a herd of elk, moose and buffalo. Monte, the antelope, and Minnie, the doe, became famous all through northern Wisconsin because of their tricks on unsuspecting guests. Wild fowls of many kinds were added and from the reserve stocks the zoos in Chicago and Cincinnati have profited, as has also the Wisconsin state game preserve.

The greatest loss to Comiskey, who has footed the bills for practically all the animals, was the departure of "Big Bill," the moose.

Bill was captured in the Rainy Lake region while still wobbling. He was brought up on a bottle at Camp Jerome and in time grew up to become one of the most magnificent antlered specimens on the continent. One night during a storm, a fallen tree leveled a section of the fence. Bill found the hole and struck out for the land of his nativity. Never deviating a hair's breadth he kept a straight line for his former home until laid low by a huntsman's bullet, much to the grief of the Old Roman, who had offered a reward of $500 for his capture.

When the big game season opened in the north Comiskey and his friends were waiting to get the first shot. A distribution of venison always followed the hunt. The jokes that Comiskey and Ban Johnson played on each other were legion. On one occasion both came near being made victims by the manager of a lumber camp in the Rainy Lake region. Awakened early one morning by the hired man the nimrods were told that a big buck was browsing in the tamarack swamp.

"Coming," answered both in unison, but Comiskey thought better of it, rolled over and went back to sleep. Johnson jumped into his hunting clothes, grabbed a rifle and, after crawling through the brush for a mile or so, spied a pair of magnificent antlers.

"You've got him," yelled the self-appointed guide with the report of the gun and, without giving Ban the benefit of a second look rushed him to the fallen monarch.

"Grab the other end of the pole," suggested Ban's companion as the head of the American League was given his first opportunity to survey the nicely suspended carcass of a deer.

Johnson had his suspicions, but kept his own counsel.

Had Comiskey not taken to baseball he could have made a living as a cook. His skill in peeling potatoes, boning a bass and skinning an onion, is second to none. He takes the greatest pleasure in superintending cooking operations and, while others have their tussles with the muskie and bass, he labors over the stewpan and coffee pot in some clearing in the brush. Having always lived in the open he is at home in the woods. But once he made a "break" which nearly cost him his life.

Going down the Flambeau River in northern Wisconsin on a summer's day he decided to cool his bare feet in the running waters. He neglected to keep his underpinnings out of the sun after the operation and by night they had swelled to twice their natural size. It was impossible to continue the journey. In pitch darkness the guide found a settler's cabin about a mile from the river. Comiskey sat up all night with his feet in a tub of buttermilk, but he had waited too long. Blood poisoning set in and it took one of Chicago's greatest specialists to save his life.

With the northern woods deep in snow and with rivers and lakes frozen up, Comiskey found an outlet for his restlessness at another point of the compass.

Fifteen years ago the much-photographed houseboat "White Sox" became a famous craft on the lower Mississippi and its tributaries. The White River of Arkansas saw it many times. It was constructed to accommodate about twenty-five persons. No one ever heard of an empty bunk on the good ship. The big idea had been originally to use the craft as a wild fowl supply boat for those who were compelled to remain at home. If the company was out of luck the southern markets did a rushing business on the return north of the tourists.

The hunting program was not elaborate. Having anchored the boat in some secluded nook along the river the hunters were told off, pits were dug, blinds erected and the slaughter was on. Once Joe Higgins, public printer of the city of Chicago and another guest sat in a pit all day waiting for geese. Decoys were scattered all about them. Soon they were surrounded with the cacklers, but in the bottom sat the two arguing over the election in the Nineteenth Ward. Spectators on the houseboat had noticed the flock through their glasses and Comiskey suggested that someone row over and help to collect the kill. The rowers frightened the geese and the noise of flapping wings disturbed the debate in the pit. The pair stuck their heads above the edge of the blind and let go all four barrels. Nothing came down, but both got a glimpse of the boat in the distance.

"Suppose they are coming for us," suggested Higgins' partner.

"No, I think not," remarked the printer. "I have an idea that Commy has sent someone to take away our guns."

Comiskey's real parties were staged at home in Chicago, usually within the "loop." There in some secluded side room would gather the choicest spirits of the city. Few had a chance to "buy" while "Commy" was around. The sessions began during the forenoon and lasted until after midnight.

As a storyteller the "Old Roman" has few peers. In these sessions day after day, night upon night, old battles of the diamond would be refought, exploits in the woods recounted and plans laid for the next venture. Any suggestion which promised a variation was eagerly taken up and thus, after an all night gathering, "Commy" and his pals were as likely as not to start on a thousand mile trip in the morning.

Comiskey's abstemious habits in his youth stood him in good stead in those days. With the members of the winter club steadily shifting, hour by hour, the head of the table looked as fresh at the finish as at the start. The conversation was always clean. No one ever tried the experiment of a salacious story or an outburst of profanity a second time within hearing of Comiskey.

One of "Commy's" most famous "hang-outs" was the "J.V.B. Club" in the Fisher Building in Chicago. To this spot drifted the

"Old Roman's" friends from all parts of the globe. The plans for some of the biggest campaigns in two baseball wars were perfected in the back room. It is doubtful if there ever was a prominent man in baseball who, at one time or another did not "sit in" during the continuous sessions, which began in 1899 and lasted for full twenty years.

♦ Chapter XVII ♦

From "Commy's" Friends

From a former baseball enemy—It does double for two more—A tribute from McGraw—Al Reach remembers "Commy" as the "greatest"—Lipton and the autographed ball—Spink and Foley recall Comiskey's early days—"Never another like him," says Joe Cantillon.

Barney Dreyfuss, owner of the Pittsburgh National League ball club, lost a fortune and his best players when the American League raided his team in 1901 and 1902. The aggressive tactics of Charles A. Comiskey were held largely responsible. Dreyfuss became a baseball enemy of the "Old Roman" yet the Pittsburgh magnate wrote this in 1919:

> Nothing could give me greater pleasure than the opportunity to express my appreciation of Charles A. Comiskey—both personally and as a baseball man. I have known him since 1885, when he managed and played first base for the famous St. Louis Browns, then owned by Chris von der Ahe.
>
> Comiskey, or "Commy," as he is more affectionately known by every one, was a great ball player, a great manager and today he is a great man in baseball affairs, but above all those things he is greater still as a man of high character.

> I am glad that I have had the pleasure of being closely acquainted with Mr. Comiskey during my thirty or more years in baseball. There is no other baseball friendship I have made in all that time that I cherish more highly than the friendship of Charles A. Comiskey. May he live long and prosper.

Charles H. Ebbets, president of the Brooklyn Club, also of the opposition, saw his greatest player, Fielder Jones, jump to the White Sox but even after that grievous blow he could express these sentiments:

> It has been my pleasure to claim the friendship of Charles Comiskey for a period of 35 years, our acquaintance having been formed in 1884, the second year of my connection with the Brooklyn Club. That friendship has firmly continued, despite some baseball differences, from that day to this. I think "Commy" has never, during the past 35 years, had a peer as a quick thinker, batter, fielder, base runner and playing manager.
>
> I well remember "Commy" in the Eighties, when, with a practically invincible team, he used to beat Brooklyn game after game. On a particular occasion which I have in mind he came to Brooklyn and gave us a "show" by switching his team around. Six-foot "Commy" went to second base and five-foot-seven Robinson to first. Latham changed places with Catcher Bushong, putting on the wind pad and mask, Bushong attempting to play third base. "Commy" assigned Hudson, his third string pitcher, to officiate in the box. All we got was a "show." Needless to say St. Louis beat Brooklyn just the same but I thought it was kind of "Commy" to give us a chance.
>
> Later on he favored Brooklyn by selling us the releases of Pitcher Caruthers for $7,500; Pitcher and First Baseman Foutz for $5,500, and Catcher Bushong for $4,500. It was the sensational deal of that period. I wish long life and prosperity to "Commy." He deserves all that he has and more, too.

XVII. *From "Commy's" Friends*

August Herrmann, president of the Cincinnati Ball Club, a power in the National League, after sixteen years of intimate relations with Comiskey, writes:

> Charles A. Comiskey's performances as a player, record as a manager, achievements as a club executive and unblemished reputation as a sportsman, have justly earned for him merited pre-eminence in the annals of the game to which he has devoted his life.
>
> Not content with his unequaled contributions to its progress and popularity in the United States, the "Old Roman" has exploited our National Game in foreign countries and he will continue his splendid services until called out by the Great Umpire.
>
> To have known and to have been associated with him is a source of pride and satisfaction to all connected with the game.

Few have had a better opportunity to size up Comiskey than John J. McGraw, now manager and vice president of the New York Giants. As a member of the Baltimore Orioles in 1891 McGraw encountered Comiskey in the American Association and in the three years following he bumped up against him while "Commy" was with the Cincinnati team. For four months the two were together in their trip around the world. In 1917 they clashed in a world's series. After an acquaintance extending over a period of twenty-eight years McGraw has formed this estimate of the "Old Roman":

> After our trip around the world the conviction was forced upon me that there was only one Comiskey. I already knew that on the ball field he had been in a class by himself, but I did not know him as a man until I had rubbed elbows with him for four months, under all kinds of trying conditions. Despite the fact that he was suffering from bodily ills during practically the

entire trip, I never heard him complain, and his cheerful disposition helped to keep the rest of us on an even keel.

In my business dealings with him he was more than fair. Liberality marked his every move. Although thousands of dollars were involved we never had the slightest difference. All he insisted on was that each team should play to win and, as he said at the finish, he had no cause to be disappointed on that score.

Comiskey was famous when I first started in. He had won four championships for the St. Louis Browns, so naturally he was a hero to me from the minute I first saw him. I admire him to-day much more than I did then for I knew him only as a player in my younger days. Now I know him as a man.

It is no disparagement to others to say that some of the greatest players in the game copied "Commy's" style of playing. He taught the first baseman how to play the position. He furnished the rest of the infielders with new strategy. He gave you the impression, wherever you happened to meet him, that he was always thinking. There was hardly a game in which he didn't spring something new. He fought for every point to the last ditch and, in common with many others of his time, seldom ran across an umpire with good eyesight. No one, however, could say that he did not battle fairly.

Comiskey had his critics but few realized that he was usually two jumps ahead of everybody else. That earned him a reputation for crabbedness on the field when, as a matter of fact, he was exactly the opposite. He never spilled a lot of words just to hear himself talk. There was no one more economical with language than Comiskey but when keyed up every word carried a barb. Years have not dulled his faculty in this respect. I know of no man who can get at the meat of an argument more quickly than the owner of the White Sox. It is for that reason that others listen to him, whether they are partners or rivals.

In his dealing with players and owners he has played the

> game on the square and in the open. He has done the same with the fans and that accounts for his hold on the followers of the game. Baseball will thrive after he is gone but there can never be another Comiskey.

Hugh Jennings, an ex-teammate of McGraw's, has also had a chance to observe him. He writes:

> Comiskey played his last season in Cincinnati my first year in the major league. I did not have much of an opportunity to observe his good qualities as a player or manager. I have known him since coming to the American League in 1907. He has always been most generous to the press and public and his executive ability, coupled with his faculty of making friends, has been of inestimable benefit to the American League, particularly in the City of Chicago.

John M. Ward, who organized the Brotherhood revolt, and was one of the game's great players, places Comiskey among the "outstanding figures in baseball." Ward is now a successful attorney in New York but he has not forgotten the old days, of which he penned the following:

> "Commy" is one of the outstanding figures in baseball. As a manager he ranks with Ned Hanlon, Connie Mack, John McGraw, Wilbert Robinson and other great player-managers. He helped to systematize the play. As a first baseman he developed the possibilities of his position. He was the first man to cut loose from the bag and play deep, leaving the pitcher to cover the bag on hits that before his time used to go safely through to right field.
>
> As a man he was always a generous opponent and a most lovable character. I have seen little of him in recent years but

> have been glad to read of his success as the president and owner of the White Sox. We have had many hard battles against one another but he was such a fair fighter in the old days that I have never lost my regard for him and shall always wish him the greatest possible measure of success.

Money is of small moment to Comiskey, according to Frank J. Navin, president and owner of the Detroit Tigers. What Mr. Navin thinks of his fellow magnate follows:

> "Commy" is a true sportsman. He is in baseball because he loves the game and for no other consideration. He has plenty of the world's goods, but I feel sure nothing could induce him to dispose of the White Sox. Money to him is only the means of accomplishing a noteworthy achievement. He would sooner be the owner of the world's best baseball club than the biggest financial giant in Wall street. The sportsmanship of the man and the deep study he has given his favorite pastime have been great factors in his success. Baseball owes a big debt to Charles A. Comiskey.

Of the scores who have contributed to this volume none has portrayed the character of Comiskey more vividly than has A. J. Reach, the millionaire sporting goods manufacturer of Philadelphia and the partner of Connie Mack. Mr. Reach helped the original Athletics to win the first championship in baseball in 1871, years before Comiskey donned a uniform but the two came to know each other intimately later on. As soon as the Philadelphia magnate was apprised of the project which this book realizes, he wrote:

> I am greatly pleased to hear that the life of Comiskey is about to be written and published. No man ever in baseball, with the possible exception of Al Spalding, has done more for the game

in all of its branches, and so deserves to have the record of his life and of his great deeds written, and thus preserved for the pleasure of this and the instruction of future generations of baseball fans. Certainly no man in baseball, past or present, has done more to deserve such a tribute and honor than Charles A. Comiskey.

I cannot speak of Comiskey as a ball player from personal contact or from the intimate angle of association on the diamond, as I was just ahead of his generation. When Comiskey first burst upon the scene along about 1882 or 1883 I had retired from active participation in the game for some years, and was devoting most of my time to a growing sporting goods business. But I kept in close touch with every phase of the game and well remember seeing Comiskey play many, many times throughout his brilliant major league career, which I have followed with interest through all the years down to this day.

As a ball player, even in that early day, he exhibited all the qualifications which made for instant success and laid the foundation for his future greatness. He played the first base position years ahead of his time and his method of playing the bag became the style which all modern first basemen must use. He was the first guardian of the initial sack who realized its fielding possibilities, and played it as deep almost as short stop. In all respects was his fielding of the position a revelation. In batting and base running he was also one of the best men of his day.

As a manager he was in a class with Harry Wright, and shared with that great manager the distinction of winning four straight pennants, something that no other manager, in any league, ever accomplished. He was a consummate handler of men; knew human nature perfectly—a faculty which by the way he retains to this day; had intimate knowledge of the strength and weakness of his players and had the ability to get the best out of all of them. He was strict with his men, yet always fair, and absolutely impartial, and this won for him the respect as well as esteem of his players. His rugged impartiality and honesty early acquired for him the sobriquet the "Old Roman," which has clung to him ever since.

Charles A. Comiskey stands out as a great national heroic figure by reason not only of his success, but also because he is the only man in the game to-day who has risen from the ranks to the position of sole club-owner in the second largest city of the country—a position which has made him probably the richest individual club owner in the country—all achieved by his own labor and effort in the face of many discouragements.

To his artistic excellence must be added other distinctions besides the winning of four consecutive pennants. I think he is the only manager or club owner who has won two World's Series in different leagues; he shares with Boston the distinction of never having lost a World's Series and he shares with Mr. Spalding the distinction of having spread the gospel of baseball over the earth by a world tour of two major league teams.

Take it all in all the baseball career of Comiskey has been wonderful, unique in many respects, and superlatively great in every way, and it is therefore entirely fitting that it should be imperishably commemorated in a printed volume, for the enlightenment and instruction of this and future generations, so that when he is gone we may justly say with the immortal bard, "We shall not look upon his like again." Meantime I sincerely hope that Comiskey may be spared for many years to come in order not only to continue his heroic work for the good of baseball, but to enjoy the well deserved prosperity and popularity that has crowned his life work.

As Mr. Reach is a veteran among owners, so is Frank C. Bancroft among the managers. "Banny" as he is best known to his friends was manager of the Providence pennant winners in 1884 when Charley Radbourne hung up his great pitching record. He is now and has been for almost a generation business manager of the Cincinnati Reds. He teamed it with "Commy" in the years 1892–93–94. This is what he has to say:

It was my good fortune to be connected with "Commy" from 1892 to 1895 as business manager of the Reds when he managed the team. No one was ever more loyal to his employers than was "Commy" to Messrs. Brush and Lloyd, who owned the club at that time. While many of the present-day managers seem to consider it a favor to play an exhibition game "Commy" told me to book as many as I could as he considered it better for the team to play than to lay idle. He was not in the best of health at that time but he played in every game scheduled.

No manager ever had the quick wit that Comiskey had. I remember on one occasion Mr. Brush and he had a conference. After it was over Mr. Brush remarked to me: "The captain missed his vocation. He should have been a lawyer."

People who knew Mr. Brush can appreciate the value of the remark as it came from a man who in legal acumen and baseball matters, in my belief, never had an equal.

The "Old Roman" originated a peculiar way of playing first base, playing deep in right and making his pitchers cover the bag when he could not reach it. We have had great first basemen since his day but none has been in his class. He was also a fighter, always leading his team, and I think he has landed more pennants than any other manager who played ball.

To my mind the American League owes its success to the brains of Charles Comiskey more than any other man living. It was "Commy" who made Ban Johnson president and no one knows better than Ban himself the value of his counsel. Comiskey has a host of friends in Cincinnati and as one of them, I voice the sentiment of all, when I say that as a man, player and friend, he never was or never will be equaled.

Al Spink was instrumental in signing Comiskey for the St. Louis Browns, as secretary of the club. Mr. Spink had seen the lean youngster play on the Chicago lots, as both were natives of Chicago. Differing from others in his judgment of "Commy" as a pitcher, he agrees with the rest as to his many other qualities. He writes:

My first view of Comiskey was in the Seventies. At that time in Chicago great interest was felt in the amateur games which were played on the prairies then surrounding the city. There were diamonds laid out at Lake and Ada, Oakley and Monroe, Harrison and Wood, Leavitt and Van Buren and at Madison street and Western avenue, on the West Side. There were other grounds; one on the North Side, where the Atlantics, later the

Aetnas, held forth, and on the South Side the home of the Pastimes.

The Actives, playing at Lake and Ada streets, the West Ends at Oakley and Monroe, the Mutuals at Leavitt and Van Burne and the Libertys at Western avenue, were the clubs I often saw Comiskey playing with. My first peep at him was when he was pitching for the Libertys at Western avenue and Madison street, in a game against the Dreadnaughts, with Ike Fleming handling his delivery.

Comiskey was then a tall, slender, serious faced lad, who sawed wood and said nothing. He pitched the ball underhanded, not with much speed, but with a very good command for that time.

It was several years after my first view of Comiskey in Chicago that Ted Sullivan brought the Dubuque Rabbits to St. Louis to play a series of games with the then co-operative Browns. I was secretary of that club and it was through my efforts that Sullivan brought the Dubuques to St. Louis to play a couple of exhibition games. They came in "Sullivan sleepers" from the Iowa town, all wearing long linen dusters.

The arrival of the team in St. Louis, June 16, 1881, was a momentous occasion for Comiskey, for while he had often played in what he considered important games before, on this day he was to appear for the first time in Sportsmans Park, a regular baseball enclosure. It was on this field and just before the game that I had an introduction to Comiskey which induced me to write him a letter the following winter, offering him a position as first baseman of the St. Louis Browns, a place which he not only accepted but which he filled with wonderful success from 1882 to 1899, inclusive.

The letter which obtained for Comiskey his first professional job was a subject of conversation not long ago when I met him in the Bards' room at Comiskey Park. Chatting about old times he said: "Al wrote me a letter in the fall of 1881, telling me that

> Von der Ahe, who then virtually owned the St. Louis Browns, was signing up ball players for that team, the nine that was to represent St. Louis in the American Association in 1882, its maiden season. Al said in his letter: 'They are paying the players from $90 to $125 a month. Make your terms as low as possible so I can clinch one of the jobs for you.'
>
> "So there could be no possible chance for an argument I put my figure at $90. I got that, however, for only one month. The second month Vondy raised it to $150."

Sir Thomas J. Lipton is a great admirer of Comiskey. The two have much in common and both are of Irish extraction. Sir Thomas is one of four in possession of a life pass to the White Sox baseball grounds. An interesting story was in circulation last winter while I was in London, England:

At the American Army-Navy baseball game played July 4, 1918, near London, King George, who was present, autographed a baseball which was subsequently auctioned off and the proceeds turned over to charity. Sir Thomas heard about it while with a party of Americans.

"I have a baseball at home which will bring more money, if put up for sale, than any ball in existence," he said. "It was presented to me in Ceylon, 1914, and it is autographed by Charles A. Comiskey."

Thomas Foley, the "Father of Billiards," knows four generations of Comiskeys. He was an intimate friend of "Honest John" Comiskey. He saw the alderman's son Charley in his first game. He knows Lou, heir of the Old Roman and he has seen Lou's daughter. With him it is, "Like father like son."

"No one could know John Comiskey," said Mr. Foley, "without loving the man. He was the highest type of gentleman. I can see no difference in his son Charles. He is a chip of the old block with his rugged honesty and pleasing personality.

XVII. From "Commy's" Friends

"I saw Comiskey play in his first games on Chicago prairies. He hasn't changed much since then except in build and years. He was as serious in his application to the game in '76 as he is today. Later as a league player and manager I knew him well. I know of no man who deserves the success which has been his as much as Charles Comiskey. They never come to the surface any better."

Ted Sullivan has generally been given the credit for the discovery of Comiskey as a ball player. At any rate the veteran organizer gave him his first paying job. The two first met 45 years ago. Sullivan had a high opinion of the "kid." The impression still remains:

> I met Charles Comiskey on the campus of a Western college where we both were students. We met again in Chicago and renewed old acquaintanceship one year after leaving school, so we have been friends in business and baseball since he was 17 years old.
>
> I saw "Commy" begin as a humble player at a salary of $75 a month with me. I saw him advance to captain of the St. Louis Browns, a team that I managed and then he succeeded me as manager. I saw him as a club owner in the Western League, a league that became the "American" afterwards and made so by the ambition and natural ability of Comiskey.
>
> He entered his native city against the protests of the National League and he did it with a boldness that has ever been his chief trait. In loftiness and purity of character, and with a sportsmanship that has given him the great quality that has endeared him to the citizens of Chicago, he stands to-day in a class by himself.
>
> He is without a taint in speech or thought; he never was guilty of a vulgar or obscene story. As a wit he is original. He stands to-day above his compeers in the National game as a mountain does above its foothills.
>
> As a ball player Comiskey was the equal of Cobb as a run-

> getter. It was when a game was close that his greatness came to the surface. To tie up a game or win it in a pinch when on the bases was his delight. Time and time again I saw him do it while playing and captaining the four-time winners of the American Association.
>
> As a first baseman he never had an equal in mentality or mechanical finish. He was the poetry of motion in receiving or fielding the ball and this, added to his magnetism and dash, made him the most finished first baseman in the history of the game.

Joe Cantillon, manager of the Minneapolis team in the American Association, found out that a story on "Commy" was being written. It interested Joe, as no one has been closer to the "Old Roman" than he. When the two did not scrap over decisions on the ball fields or, later, over trades, they usually were fishing or hunting together. As a story teller Joe is second only to the owner of the White Sox. In his own inimitable style he sat down and wrote twenty pages of reminiscences to the author, the longest letter he ever indited. Some of the material has been incorporated in other parts of the book. His closing sentence has not. It is:

"There will never, never be another 'Commy,' so go as strong as you can."

This homely tribute, we believe, came from the heart. Others, it seems, have been dictated by similar emotions. Had they not, there would have been no chapter on "appreciation," nor could it have been added:

"He played no favorites."

"He never hit below the belt."

♦ CHAPTER XVIII ♦

A Pen Picture of the "Old Roman"

Life is one of epigrams—Comiskey never saw a popular auditor—Cuts his cloth according to means—Queer experiences with ball players—Umpires as he saw them—Sun glasses and a $6 mattress—Puts aside the crown—World does not owe him a living.

Analyzing Comiskey's character is a task for the psychologist. The author of this book and numerous contributors have touched upon some of his traits, but merely as observers. What follows may not adequately portray his many-sided nature but it will help to tint the picture.

Comiskey's life has been one of epigrams. Incisive irony and wit have punctuated his speech on the field and around the council table. Pointed retorts have disarmed opponents. A terse comment has often swung a big business deal. He has always hit straight from the shoulder with singleness of purpose but even though hewing to the line, caution has ever dictated the distribution of the chips.

He has avoided the complex in life. With him it has been aiming at the bull's eye. His vision has been straight ahead. Sometimes he has left the impression that he permitted his affairs to drift with the stream, but at the same time no one ever noticed that he picked out the wrong landing place. Again he has shown traits of inconsistency. He has been given credit for having a well balanced mind but some allege he has amassed a fortune without a system.

Rivals of Comiskey insist that he is a keen business man—one of the shrewdest in the game—yet the needs have always determined the daily procedure in the conduct of his own affairs. During his first ten years in Chicago he got along without the services of a bookkeeper. Charles Fredericks, a nephew who combined the duties of secretary and treasurer of the White Sox club, kept the office ledger in his inside coat pocket. Each year he had to invest fifteen cents for a new book, but not a penny went astray. The handling of the funds was simplicity itself. Each day's receipts were dumped into a satchel and taken to a downtown bank. Necessary payments were made by check. What was left at the end of the season was reckoned as profits.

A friend of Comiskey suggested the employment of an efficiency expert for his office, after he had moved into the quarters he now occupies.

"I don't need him," said Comiskey. "It isn't system that the fans want. They want seats and good ball games. I never saw a popular auditor yet."

The lack of system did not prevent him from running his club on business principles. His players received what they were worth when they first signed. If they lasted perhaps they got more than they could earn in time. Gossip had it that he was "free with his friends but 'close' with his ball players." There is a heap o' truth in the first. The fact that not a single one of his players jumped to the Federal League gives the lie to the second.

Comiskey's fixed principle was always to gauge the outlay for ball players by his receipts. If the income did not match the expenses the team would be trimmed down. Thus, he did not start out as an owner with special trains nor put up in the finest hotels. As soon as the bank roll permitted, nothing was too good for his men.

"The man who does not keep track of the pay roll has no business in baseball," he said once when told that a major league magnate had gone broke.

How he cut his cloth according to his means was illustrated while he was in St. Paul. He had a chance to buy Chauncey Fisher from the Cincinnati Club. Joe Cantillon was the biggest booster for the pitcher.

"He would be a great man for your league and you should get him," urged Cantillon.

"But he wants $275 a month," interposed Comiskey.

"Well, he is worth it to you," insisted Joe.

"Is he if I don't take in the money at the gate?" queried Commy.

Comiskey had little patience with the player who developed expensive tastes with the growth of the game. Once he was apprised that one of his star players was going to quit unless he was given an increase over his $10,000 salary.

"So he is going to quit, is he?" mused Comiskey. "When I was playing ball I was always afraid that the game was going to quit me."

Although the owner of the Sox encouraged saving on the part of his men he was as little enamored of the miser as of the spendthrift or the aristocratic hold-out. Starting his career in "Sullivan sleepers," which meant the day coach, he never has been able to fully appreciate the idiosyncrasies of modern ball players. It has always been a puzzle to him why a player who at home thought he was wasting his own money if he paid more than $5 a week at a boarding house should roar at an "upper" or protest against not getting a front room on the parlor floor.

On a training trip one spring the team stopped at the best hotel in New Orleans. The third day one of the players, who had been known to do his own cooking at home, announced that he was going to quit. He was asked why.

"I can't stand the eats," was his reply.

In the early days the players were given $3 a day for meals while on trains. One of the men on a trip to Boston left Chicago with $1.50 in his pocket. He arrived with $3.50, but roared because the caviar served at the hotel was not to his liking.

On the first training trip of the Sox to California the team was put up at what was considered the best and highest priced hotel in San Francisco. It had such a reputation for exclusiveness that John I. Taylor, then owner of the Boston Red Sox had offered to wager $100 with Comiskey that he couldn't get in. On the team at the time was a big raw-boned rookie. After having enjoyed the hospitality of the place for two days the recruit threatened to leave.

"What's the trouble?" asked Comiskey.

"Why, he complains because it is too swell and that there are too many rugs in the lobby. He slipped on one and sprained his ankle," explained the manager.

Comiskey still remembers one player who didn't kick. Coming up from Texas one spring the team had to take potluck in a second rate Oklahoma hotel. Everybody kicked and the gang didn't care how far their voices carried. "Tex" Jones, a lanky Kansan, was trying out with the team. After he had listened to the conversation in the dining room a few times he stopped all arguments with this:

"I haven't any license to kick. It is better than I get at home."

The hospital list on a modern ball team is another thing the "Old Roman" is unable to fathom.

Having been educated in a school where hard knocks were the daily program and where a ball team was made up of ten or twelve men, he occasionally fails properly to sympathize with the "injured" player.

Homecoming banquet at the conclusion of the world tour—Congress Hotel, Chicago, March 10, 1914.

"When I was in the game I didn't dare to stay out for fear that somebody would get my job," he said in discussing the tendency of high priced athletes to lay off on the least provocation.

Several years ago John Anderson cavorted around first base and in the outfield with the White Sox. Comiskey found it to the advantage of the team to carry an extra man while Anderson was incapacitated by reason of sickness or spitball pitchers, either of which put him on the sidelines. Following one season Comiskey was on an outing when he received a letter from Anderson asking a $3,000 salary.

"Pretty strong," suggested Commy's companion.

"Yes, it is," said Comiskey after a pause, "but maybe John is going to pay the substitute himself."

Being of a restless disposition and always up and doing, it grated on "Commy's" nerves to see extra players do nothing but take on weight. When manager of the Cincinnati team Morgan Murphy caught practically all the games, according to Frank Bancroft. This left Harry Vaughn, the second backstop on the bench most of the time. Spotting Harry at the end of the board during a sizzling game he said:

"Harry, I don't want to overwork you, but will you please carry the mask and chest protector to Morgan."

Joe Cantillon came out to the Sox ball park the morning of the first game between the Sox and Cubs for the world's championship in 1906. Joe wanted a tip on the chances of the South Siders and noticing a bandage on a player's hand, asked "Commy" about it.

"I don't know why he is wearing it, but I suppose he has heard that we are going to play him today," was Comiskey's response.

Being a past master of irony the players usually dodged him after a blunder. Sometimes the field was too small for this maneuver. Scott Stratton of the St. Paul team found it so after he had taken three healthy swings as a pinch hitter.

"I did the very best I could," mumbled Stratton on his return.

"Yes, I think you did, Scott, but I did the very worst in sending you up," said Comiskey.

That hard-loser streak in his makeup usually cropped out in every game. What the players missed in sarcasm the umpires caught. Joe Cantillon, then an umpire and "winter friend" of Commy, "stopped" most of the verbal attacks, probably because "Commy" enjoyed his repartee, for which he was noted. Once in St. Paul, when Detroit was leading the Saints 16 to 0 in the eighth inning Joe called the game on account of darkness. Comiskey accosted him.

"Why did you call the game?" demanded the irate manager.

"You didn't think you had a chance to win it, did you?" retorted the umpire.

"No, not after you had called it," responded Comiskey.

"In a series of games between St. Paul and Minneapolis, always bitterly fought," relates Cantillon, "President Johnson sent up an extra umpire to help me out. We opened up at St. Paul and my assistant being a strictly 'home' umpire started in to trim Minneapolis right and left. I was roasted to a turn while everybody cheered the newcomer.

"On the following day we played in Minneapolis and Ban's arbitrator reversed his tactics of the day before. As decision after decision went against St. Paul, 'Commy' finally yelled:

"'Joe, are you going to stand for that crook trimming me in this way?'

"Well, your people cheered him all day yesterday," I answered.

"'That's all right, Joe,' said Comiskey, 'He will be a great man for me again tomorrow, but I want you to take care of me today.'"

All the irony was not vented on the umpires. While Jimmy Callahan was manager, John Collins, the veteran right fielder, fell as he was getting set to catch a long fly in an important game. The mishap cost two runs. Collins had new sun goggles, the purchase of which Comiskey had authorized.

When the manager entered the Old Roman's office the following morning he was greeted with:

"Well, I got that bill of $9 for Collins' sun glasses, all right. While you were about it why didn't you add $6 more and get him a mattress."

On the whole, taking into consideration aesthetic tastes and other peculiarities, Comiskey has less trouble with his players than perhaps any other owner in the game. The reason is because he plays no favorites. He alone is the judge of the worth of the man he signs and after one contract there is seldom any grounds for complaints. The player depends on Comiskey for a square deal and if he delivers, he knows that he is going to get everything that is coming to him.

A similar policy marks "Commy's" affairs outside of his ball club. Ever since he first started to make "copy" for the newspapers there has been much mystery why he should get so much publicity. There is no secret about it. He has furnished news fit to print, has treated the cub reporter with as much consideration as the veteran, has been without an "organ," and has never asked for a retraction.

"Print the story first and then have Commy confirm it," has been the rule among newspaper men whenever anyone has thought that he had an exclusive item. If the opposite tack were pursued Commy would be certain to call up all the rest of the "boys" and it would no longer be a "scoop." To deny a yarn because it was not true or because it didn't please him, never entered his mind. Pressed for an explanation he would find refuge in, "Well, it must be right. The Bazoo says so." If on the other hand the truth or falsity of a report needed clearing up, a "Comiskey statement" would stand the test. Never an equivocation. It was either "yes" or "no." These are the reasons why he has broken into print more often, perhaps, than any other man in the game.

Although perhaps art did not appeal to Comiskey as strongly as a .300 slugger there could be no doubt of his appreciation of its utilitarian advantages. While walking through the National Museum at Naples, Italy, he paused in front of the heroic statue of Hercules. He permitted his eyes to roam admiringly over the massive figure until they rested on the huge club which had done such execution in the Theban and Cretan leagues, and mused:

"What a pinch hitter he would have made!"

Comiskey is fair game for the joker, but he has made it a practice never to "kid" himself.

"Why not mayor of Chicago?" was the query propounded to the "Old Roman" by influential politicians, who several years ago decided that the owner of the White Sox would poll a vote commensurate with his popularity.

"I would rather win a pennant than an election," was the answer.

He explained that he was a baseball man first, last and all the time, and that politics and the game did not mix.

The subject of this sketch is not without his faults, but his worst would seem as virtues to many. He is prone to exaggerate a personal slight and to enlarge upon the motives of whose with whom he disagrees. He is sensitive as regards his own honor and reputation. Considering his mental bent, this is but natural, as he himself insists in playing all the cards above the table.

In a fight he is uncompromising if he thinks he is right. He will have to be "shown" to be proven wrong. He is a hard loser, but a generous opponent. He will go the limit for a friend, but it will take much persuasion to make him forget an injury.

He is considerate to the last degree, but knows how to insist upon his rights. He is original, but without mannerisms. He is a mixer and spender, but knows the value of money.

Comiskey's personal magnetism gains him friends wherever he goes but he holds them because he is human. He is a good judge of his fellow men but occasionally falls a prey to the designing. He has little patience with the non-producer and this has given him the reputation of a hard task master. He is a self-made man and, like his kind, expects much from others. He is independent in means, habits and thoughts, standing on his own feet. What sets him apart from those who enjoy his hospitality is that the chief tenet in his creed is that the world does NOT OWE him a living.

"Commy"

From the beginning he has been walking in the open. He has simple tastes, living most of his life in a cottage or a "flat," but he has spent a quarter of million dollars on his friends. "To buy" has been a privilege with him that he has been chary to accord to others.

Physically "Commy" is of the upstanding type—six feet in height. His facial contour helped to bestow upon him the appellation "Old Roman." He can now be classed among the heavyweights, but he was not always so. When playing ball, altitude was all he could boast of. When he wanted to make a "front" as an athlete he thrust his nether limbs into two pairs of heavy stockings and even then no bulging calves showed.

In middle life an abundance of black, wavy locks gave him the appearance of Edwin Booth. His hair is more sparse now, but his forehead has not receded. For years he has affected a gray hat of distinctive shape, the headpiece matching in color a pair of piercing eyes. It is the "Old Gray Bonnet" that the Bards sing about. They also set the story of the "Homeplate" to music.

The "Homeplate" is a cottage up in the woods, presented to the "Old Roman" a few years ago by hundreds of friends who have partaken of his hospitality. A Chicago judge made the presentation speech. "Commy" responded. He stood on a tree stump in delivering it. I only remember one thing that he said. I couldn't forget that. It was the index to his character. I believe it was from the heart. It was:

"All my life I have tried to be on the square with myself."

◆ CHAPTER XIX ◆

By "Commy" Himself

It is fitting that the man who has furnished the subject matter for the preceding chapters should have a hearing on his own account. Up to this time he has had a chance only to vouch for the facts, so permit the "Old Roman" to speak for himself:

By Charles A. Comiskey.

Having a biography prepared has always seemed to me as either superfluous or in the nature of an epitaph. The omission of both sometimes would seem to be of an advantage to the living. Also the "story" of a man should denote some achievement. I hope that what I have accomplished has been in the open, so it cannot be considered new. If it has not been out of the commonplace it should not be called noteworthy. Others have done as much as well, so I must consider it a special compliment of the author and publisher to have taken the chance they have in producing this book.

I can furnish no secret documents from hidden archives but I can make the statement that the world has given me a square deal—possibly more than I am entitled to. I can think of no exception. It has been all the same whether I have been a temporary or a permanent guests in any community in which I have lived.

"Commy"

I was perfectly satisfied with the West Side of Chicago when I was in knickerbockers. I hope it was with me. They treated me fine in Milwaukee, in Elgin and Dubuque. No one could have been given more consideration that I was in St. Louis. It is impossible to register a kick against Cincinnati and it is with pleasure that I recall my five-year stay in St. Paul. I think I left with a fair share of the population my friends.

Naturally Chicago has seemed different to me from the rest. It has never ceased to be my home. I was born here and here I hope to finish. If the people think as much of me as I do of them there can be no grounds for disagreement. There is no sectional feeling in my allegiance to the city of my birth because there happens to be a White Sox family on the South Side. I have as many personal friends on the West and North sides as I have on the South.

Words cannot express my real feelings towards the people of Chicago. Did I have the power of expression that others possess I would completely fail in voicing my appreciation of what they have done for me. They encouraged me when I first came to the city. Since then they have built a ball park for me and made it possible for me to get together teams which, at different times, have been fortunate enough to repay them for their outlay. Not I or my managers have won pennants for Chicago. The fans alone have raised the flags which have flown on the South Side.

Occasionally I have been charged with the crime of "buying" pennants. If I am guilty it has been for the sake of those who furnished the money. I have been counted a hard loser. My friends wanted me to have a winner. The fans have insisted upon it. The winning of individual ball games contributes to the total and without more victories at the end of the season than anyone else there would have been no championships.

I have fought for every point because, through bitter experience,

I early learned that one lost decision sometimes may mean the loss of a pennant. It is the small things in life which count; it is the inconsequential leak which empties the biggest reservoir.

Many have spoken about my luck. I admit that I have been fortunate in many of my undertakings but I do not think that success is governed by the throw of the dice. I do not claim that I have been more foresighted than others. I have had my reverses but I have tried not to lose my appetite.

The real secret of my good luck has been that I could always figure on support. You can do wonders when you have everybody with you. I may not be able to figure out why my friends have been with me but they have. Perhaps it is because I have tried to be on the level with them. That should not be a source of pride to me as it is part of good business. No one has any license to brag because he is honest. That should be natural instinct and, besides, if you are not, they put you in jail. Honesty is merely a form of insurance.

I have been given credit, sometimes entirely unearned, for doing many things for the advancement of the game. I have fought for it because the game deserved it. Baseball is the greatest sport in the world. It is the cleanest, besides affording more people the right kind of amusement than any other. I do not say that because I have made my living at it. I say it from the heart. There have been reports now and then that I contemplate disposing of my ball club. I never had any such intentions. I would be lost without my team. I have spent my life in the game and I have no regrets. To me it has not been misspent.

Formerly sport was not regarded as a proper calling for young men. It is beginning to assume its rightful place in society. To me baseball is as honorable as any other business. It is the most honest pastime in the world. It has to be or it could not last a season out. Crookedness and baseball do not mix. It has become immeasurably more popular as the years have gone by. It will be greater yet. This year, 1919, is the greatest season of them all.

The reason for the popularity of the sport is that it fits in with the temperament of the American people and because it is on the square. Everything is done in the open. What the magnates do behind the screens the fans care nothing about.

Year by year a higher and higher class of players come into the game. This is not meant as a slur on those of the earlier days, the pioneers, but it is a proof of the attraction it has for young men. The rewards of today are, of course, more in keeping with the efforts than was the case when I broke into the game. I started in at $3 a day. Now some players get that much a minute, counting their actual playing time.

As to a comparison between the players of my days and today there is no way of arriving at a conclusion. It is quite possible to pick a "greatest team," but the selection would be based purely on personal opinion. I think I had wonderful players in Caruthers, Foutz, Bill Gleason, O'Neill, Bushong and others, but it would be a matter of opinion to compare these with such stars as Ed Walsh, Billy Sullivan, Jiggs Donohue, Joe Jackson, Happy Felsch, Eddie Collins, Ray Schalk, Eddie Cicotte and a score or more equally as good who have played for me on my Chicago teams.

We have Ty Cobb, Walter Johnson, Christy Mathewson, Babe Ruth, Grover Alexander, and a host of others. How would they have stacked up with Radbourne, Sweeney, Ramsey, Williamson, Barnes, Pfeffer, Anson, Clarkson, Kelly, and such outstanding figures? It is hard to tell. Batting averages and pitching records do not give the answer, as conditions under which they played were different from those of today.

Personally I think Ty Cobb of the Detroit team is the greatest player of all time. This is no disparagement to others. Ty is in a class by himself. He is a wonderful batter and would have been able to hit any kind of pitching in the old days as well. He is one of the speediest men in the game. He is as good a fielder as one would want, but above all he is a thinker when in the game. His mind works every minute and he carries the team along with him.

In sportsmanship there is little to differentiate the Eighties from the present. We fought to win then. The right kind of team does so now. Perhaps we were a little rougher about it than they are now and it seemed that we could stand harder knocks then than can players of today. I do not mean that the boys have less grit today. I have some of the gamest players in the world on my own team, but then there was less arnica on tap.

The spirit of the game remains the same and that is why I take pride in being identified with it. With me baseball will never grow old. In my own estimation it may not have improved so much as many believe, but regardless of everything it is the same good old game. If I have contributed to its success I do not refer to this in the sense of boasting. I had to or fall out of the ranks. It was a fast game when I played it and the pace was hot. As the fans know, I have often had trouble in keeping up with it since then, but they have been forebearing. What I have tried to do has been my level best.

THE END.

Index

The original edition did not have an index; this one was created by the series editors

Index

Index

Index

Index

Index

Index

Index

Index